BIOMES

Discover the Earth's Ecosystems
with Environmental Science Activities for Kids

Donna Latham
Illustrated by Tom Casteel

Titles in the **Environmental Science** book set

Check out more titles at www.nomadpress.net

Nomad Press
A division of Nomad Communications
10 9 8 7 6 5 4 3 2 1

This book was manufactured by CGB Printers,
North Mankato, Minnesota, United States
March 2019, Job #265266

ISBN Softcover: 978-1-61930-739-1
ISBN Hardcover: 978-1-61930-736-0

Educational Consultant, Marla Conn

Questions regarding the ordering of this book should be addressed to
Nomad Press
2456 Christian St.
White River Junction, VT 05001
www.nomadpress.net

Contents

Interested in Primary Sources?

Look for this icon. Use a smartphone or tablet app to scan the QR code and explore more! Photos are also primary sources because a photograph takes a picture at the moment something happens.

PS You can find a list of URLs on the Resources page. If the QR code doesn't work, try searching the internet with the Keyword Prompts to find other helpful sources.

🔎 biomes

CONIFEROUS
FOREST

TEMPERATE
GRASSLAND

DECIDUOUS
FOREST

MOUNTAIN

DESERT

TUNDRA

TROPICAL SAVANNA

TROPICAL RAINFOREST

OCEAN

GREETINGS,
ECO EXPLORER!

Grab your backpack! You're about to embark on an exciting expedition to explore Earth's major biomes!

A biome is a life zone. It's a large natural area with a distinctive **climate** and **geology**, and specific water **resources**. Each biome features its own **biodiversity**, a range of living things ideally suited for life in that **environment**. There are **terrestrial** biomes on land and **aquatic** biomes in water.

Some scientists say there are five different biomes on planet Earth, and others break these biomes down into even smaller categories. In this book, we'll explore nine different biomes.

ESSENTIAL QUESTION

What type of biome do you live in?

WORDS TO KNOW

biome: a large natural area with a distinctive climate, geology, set of water resources, and plants and animals that are adapted for life there.

climate: average weather patterns in an area during a period of many years.

geology: the rocks, minerals, and physical structure of an area.

resource: anything people use to take care of themselves, such as water and food.

biodiversity: the range of living things in an ecosystem.

environment: everything in nature, living and nonliving, including plants, animals, soil, rocks, and water.

terrestrial: related to land.

aquatic: related to water.

biosphere: the area of the earth and its atmosphere inhabited by living things.

atmosphere: the blanket of air surrounding the earth.

ecosystem: an interdependent community of living and nonliving things and their environment.

habitat: a plant or animal's home, which supplies it with food, water, and shelter.

ecology: the study of the relationship between living things and their environment.

Even biomes that you might think are similar can actually be homes for very different plants and animals. For example, forests cover about a quarter of the planet. Yet different locations and climates mean you'll bound alongside snowshoe hares in one forest biome and leap with red-eyed tree frogs in another.

ONE EARTH, MANY BIOMES

The **biosphere** is the area of the earth and its **atmosphere** that is inhabited by animals and plants that depend on one another for survival. Biomes are subsections, or smaller parts, of the biosphere. Within each biome, you'll find many **ecosystems**. An interconnected balance ensures that living things survive and thrive.

Visualize a skateboard. It's built of different connected parts that work together to keep you rolling along. What happens when a ball bearing flies off? The wheel pops off. The skateboard skids to a halt. When one part fails, the whole skateboard is affected.

An ecosystem works the same way—all the living and nonliving things in it depend on one another.

DID YOU KNOW?

The prefix eco comes from the Greek word *oikos*, meaning "house." Eco refers to environments or **habitats**. For example, **ecology** is the study of the relationship between living things and their environment. Ecologists study ecology. What other words do you know that contain eco?

Death Valley, a desert that stretches across California and Nevada, is home to many different plants and animals that depend on each other for survival in harsh conditions.

WORDS TO KNOW

interdependent: relying on each other.

savanna: a dry, rolling grassland with scattered shrubs and trees.

desert: the hottest biome, with very little rain, less than 10 inches per year.

coniferous: describes cone-bearing shrubs and trees, often with needles for leaves. Coniferous trees do not lose their leaves each year.

tundra: a treeless Arctic region that is permanently frozen below the top layer of soil.

sandstorm: a strong wind carrying clouds of sand with it, especially in a desert.

plume: when a material spreads out into a shape that resembles a feather.

torrential: a sudden, violent outpouring.

Living things are plants and animals, while nonliving things include the sun, air, rocks, soil, and water. All parts of the ecosystem interact with their environment and with each other. Teamwork keeps complex, **interdependent** systems balanced and working.

Earth's biomes are connected together, creating a vast web of life. As they sprawl across the globe, biomes overlap and blend together. For example, tropical **savannas** mingle with **deserts**, and **coniferous** forests spill into **tundra**.

When natural or manmade disasters such as volcanic eruptions or oil spills take place in one biome, they often have an effect upon other biomes as well.

IMAGINE THIS SKATEBOARD IS A BIOME.

AND ALL ITS DIFFERENT MOVING PIECES ARE PARTS OF THE BIOME, LIKE DIFFERENT ECOSYSTEMS.

IF ONE LITTLE BALL BEARING IS MISSING, THEN THE WHEEL STOPS WORKING AND THEN....

I GET IT! IF ONE PART GETS MESSED UP THEN THE WHOLE THING MIGHT NOT WORK RIGHT.

EXACTLY!

WELL, THAT SOUNDS REALLY DANGEROUS....

THE LAST TIME I TRIED RIDING A BIOME I SPRAINED MY WRIST!

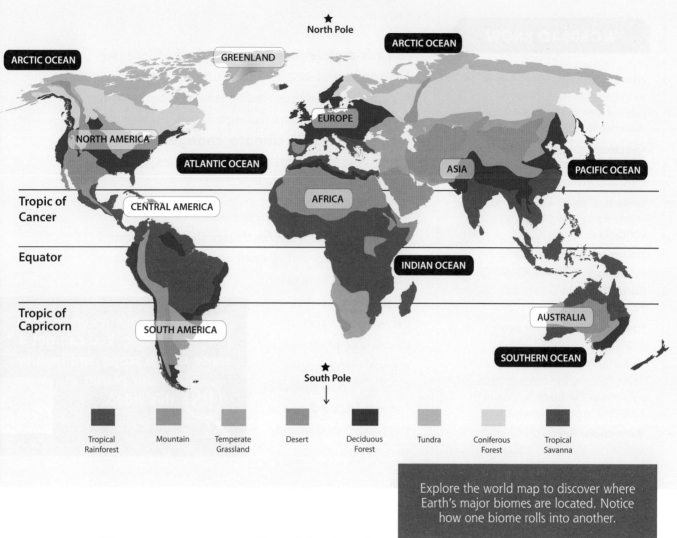

★
North Pole

ARCTIC OCEAN

ARCTIC OCEAN

GREENLAND

EUROPE

NORTH AMERICA

ATLANTIC OCEAN

ASIA

PACIFIC OCEAN

Tropic of
Cancer

CENTRAL AMERICA

AFRICA

Equator

INDIAN OCEAN

Tropic of
Capricorn

AUSTRALIA

SOUTH AMERICA

SOUTHERN OCEAN

★
South Pole

| Tropical Rainforest | Mountain | Temperate Grassland | Desert | Deciduous Forest | Tundra | Coniferous Forest | Tropical Savanna |

Explore the world map to discover where Earth's major biomes are located. Notice how one biome rolls into another.

Have you ever set up a line of dominoes? If you knock over one domino, it knocks down the second one. The second one knocks down the third one, and so on. Whenever something happens in one biome, it launches a similar domino effect. The change sweeps through other biomes.

Imagine a massive **sandstorm** as it whirls across Africa's Sahara Desert. A huge, hazy dust **plume** billows higher and higher into the sky. Winds blow the dust across the Atlantic Ocean. When the wandering cloud blots out the sun, it cools ocean waters. This can cause a tropical storm to develop. **Torrential** rains and violent winds then clobber the Gulf Coast of Florida— all because of a sandstorm in Africa!

WORDS TO KNOW

climate change: a change in long-term weather patterns, which can happen through natural or man-made processes.

species: a group of living things that are closely related and can produce offspring.

adapt: to make a change in response to new or different conditions.

circumnavigate: to travel completely around something.

flora: the plant life in an ecosystem.

fauna: the animal life in an ecosystem.

turf: the grass and the layer of earth held by the grass roots. Can also mean the place someone resides and feels ownership of.

extinction: the death of an entire species so that it no longer exists.

Let's explore more of these places! Get ready for a wild and woolly adventure in extreme regions. You'll zip across continents, hover over volcanoes, and creep through brush. Along the way, you'll explore **climate change** and learn about environmental threats to biomes, as well as what you can do to help.

In this book, you'll read about factors that determine which living things inhabit a biome. You'll dig into soil, a critical component that controls the types of plants that grow there. You'll encounter plants and animals and learn how different **species** have **adapted** to the particular conditions of their biome.

The variety of biomes on Earth is pretty impressive. **You can get a sense of the scope and beauty of our planet in this video.**

🔎 Gregorio intro biomes

How have these Adelie penguins adapted to harsh conditions in Antarctica?

credit: Jason Auch (CC BY 2.0)

First, wander the planet's magnificent forests. Then, battle the blazing sun and scorching temperatures in sizzling desert areas. Later, shiver in Earth's frigid, desolate regions. Many of these places are downright hostile to living things such as you!

As you **circumnavigate** the globe, you'll learn about **flora** and **fauna** in each biome. Plants and animals are perfectly built for survival on their home **turf**. Along your way, meet some of the world's precious endangered animals, and discover why they face **extinction**. Ready to go? We're off!

Good Science Practices

Every good scientist keeps a science journal!

Scientists use the scientific method to keep their experiments organized. Choose a notebook to use as your science journal. As you read through this book and do the activities, keep track of your observations and record each step in a scientific method worksheet, like the one shown here.

Each chapter of this book begins with an essential question to help guide your exploration of biomes and the environment. Keep the question in your mind as you read the chapter. At the end of each chapter, use your science journal to record your thoughts and answers.

Question: What are we trying to find out? What problem are we trying to solve?
Research: What is already known about the problem?
Hypothesis/Prediction: What do we think the answer will be?
Equipment: What supplies are we using?
Method: What procedure are we following?
Results: What happened? Why?

ESSENTIAL QUESTION

What type of biome do you live in?

MAKE A PAPIER-MÂCHÉ GLOBE

Earth isn't just your home. It also provides the precious **natural resources** you need for survival. Our planet seems huge and **invincible**. Yet the earth is surprisingly **vulnerable**, and it's our job to take care of it. A globe is a three-dimensional model of the earth that includes its continents and oceans. You can use a globe to refer to when learning about the different biomes in the world. This project will take several days or more to complete.

❯ **Use your favorite recipe for a papier-mâché paste and strips of newspaper to completely cover an inflated balloon.** Remember to tie a string to the bottom of the balloon. Set the balloon aside and allow it to dry for several days.

❯ **When the globe is dry, pop the balloon with a needle.** Gently tug the string to remove the balloon from the globe.

❯ **Do some research and find a map or globe to refer to so you can locate continents and oceans.** Sketch continent boundaries on your dried globe. You might want to practice on a sheet of paper first! Paint the continents green and the oceans blue. It's a good idea to paint continents first, let them dry overnight, and then paint oceans so the colors won't ooze together.

❯ **Allow the globe to dry for at least 24 hours.** When it's totally dry, use a marker to label continents and oceans. Select a special spot to display your globe.

Try This!

As you learn about the different biomes throughout this book, locate them on your globe. Can you think of a creative way to label them?

WORDS TO KNOW

natural resource: a material such as coal, timber, water, or land that is found in nature and is useful to humans.

invincible: something that cannot be defeated.

vulnerable: susceptible to emotional or physical harm.

Chapter 1

HOME
SWEET HOME

Earth is the only planet we know of that can sustain life. Animals and plants inhabit nearly every nook and cranny of the global ecosystem. Organisms are everywhere!

Humans enjoy a cozy partnership with the planet. Earth provides us with precious resources. In return, we must be good **stewards** and use resources wisely to protect our planet.

What do living things require for survival? They rely on the sun's energy, light, and heat. They depend on water, food, and the atmosphere, which contains the necessary **elements** of oxygen, carbon dioxide, and nitrogen.

ESSENTIAL QUESTION

How does Earth sustain life?

WORDS TO KNOW

sustain: to provide support.

organism: any living thing, such as a plant or animal.

steward: a person who looks after something, such as the environment.

element: a basic substance, such as gold or oxygen, made of only one kind of atom.

lichen: a plant-like organism made of algae and fungus that grows on solid surfaces such as rocks or trees.

bountiful: large in quantity.

ecoregion: a large area, smaller than a biome, that has its own climate, geology, plants, and animals.

transformation: a dramatic or extreme change.

drought: a long period of little or no rain.

marsh: an inland area of wet, low land.

YOUR HOME TURF

Go outside and look around. Do you spot prickly pears, gently swaying palm trees, or patchy **lichens**? Do you hear waves lapping onshore or the buzz of bustling city streets? Which birds do you observe—honking geese flying in V formation, gobbling wild turkeys, or squabbling pelicans? What's scuttling over land—iguanas, Key Largo wood rats, squirrels and deer, or wadded clumps of paper that pollute the streets?

Notice how your area or neighborhood flows. Does one cornfield roll into another? Do streets with houses, apartment buildings, and shops connect to roads with parks and schools?

As life zones, biomes are Earth's communities. If you could hover above the planet like a hummingbird, you'd notice that each biome blends into another.

How many biomes does our **bountiful** planet have? That's debatable. Some scientists divide the planet into five biomes. Others split it into 20. Still others think it's more accurate to divide Earth into hundreds of **ecoregions**.

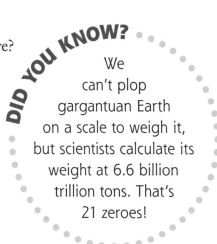

DID YOU KNOW?

We can't plop gargantuan Earth on a scale to weigh it, but scientists calculate its weight at 6.6 billion trillion tons. That's 21 zeroes!

BIOMES, THEY ARE A CHANGIN'

One fact is certain—biomes are constantly changing. From Earth's earliest history, biomes have undergone **transformation**. Change happens for different reasons, including natural events, human impact, and climate change.

Natural events have always played a role in the transformation of biomes. For example, floodwaters washed away coastal areas in Louisiana and Texas. In other areas, such as Grand Pointe Prairie County in Alberta, Canada, **droughts** turned rich soil into cracked fields and shriveled farmers' crops.

Humans have changed things, too. As people settled in different areas, they required shelter and food to survive. People cleared forests to create space for homes and farmland. As populations boomed, people drained swamps and **marshes** to plant more crops, build businesses, and construct roads. They hunted animals to feed growing families and to provide furs to trade.

Check It Out!

What's the planet's population right now? Which are the 10 most populous countries on Earth? Answers are a click away! Explore the U.S. Census Bureau's U.S. and World Population Clock. The site provides a wealth of information.

 You can find the rates of birth and death and population estimates plus explore interactive charts and graphs.

🔎 census population clock

WORDS TO KNOW

conserve: to save or protect something, or to use it carefully so it isn't used up.

endure: to experience for a long time.

trait: a specific characteristic of an organism.

mammal: a type of animal, such as a human, dog, or cat. Mammals are born live, feed milk to their young, and usually have hair or fur covering most of their skin.

ravenous: starving.

predator: an animal or plant that kills and eats another animal.

adaptation: something about a plant or animal that helps it survive in its habitat.

Climate change greatly impacts biomes. It can be tricky to maintain a balanced partnership with our planet. Earth's growing population, which is galloping toward a whopping 8 billion people, uses more and more of Earth's resources. Many people treat our world with great care. But others don't.

Our behavior can affect the environment and cause great harm.

Scientists continue to study the environment and the ways humans affect our planet. Worldwide, nearly 97 percent of scientists believe human activities have caused sweeping changes on Earth. Climate change is a critical topic. Science professionals point to overwhelming evidence that indicate our planet is warming at a rapid, alarming rate.

Today, people are increasingly aware of the delicate balance of life on Earth. Many groups are devoted to **conserving** the planet's natural resources and preserving biomes.

As you read and explore this book, ponder the environmental threats that place our biomes and our planet at risk. Consider your own role in the world. Ask yourself how you can play a part to keep Earth thriving.

PERFECTLY ADAPTED!

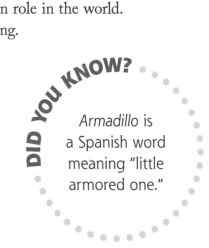

DID YOU KNOW?

Armadillo is a Spanish word meaning "little armored one."

When you imagine a desert, you probably don't think of a furry polar bear. That burly beast couldn't survive such extreme heat. And the Arctic isn't where you'd expect to find an armor-plated armadillo. It's simply not built to **endure** frigid conditions.

Play Ball!

Adaptive **traits** allow animals to thrive and survive. Consider the amazing armadillo, a small burrowing **mammal**. It's physically adapted with hard-plated armor formed of bone and horn. This shell shields the armadillo's head, back, legs, and tail. What happens when a **ravenous predator** approaches? Some armadillos roll into tight balls! This behavioral **adaptation** protects their soft bellies from fierce jaws.

WORDS TO KNOW

valve: a structure that controls the passage of fluid through a tube.

putrid: decaying and smelling bad.

pollen: a fine, yellow powder produced by flowering plants. Pollen is spread around by the wind, birds, and insects, and is needed by a flower to make a seed.

Through adaptation, animals develop the right kind of physical features and behaviors to survive in their habitats, or homes.

They've adapted to live with the climate, build homes, steer clear of predators, and attract mates.

Aquatic animals, such as beavers, are adapted for life in water. When busy beavers build underwater lodges, they seal their eyes and noses shut with a special **valve**. They flap hefty, webbed feet to swim. Beavers are just right for water work.

Plants are also adapted for survival. Try catching a whiff of the endangered corpse lily, found in the rainforests of Sumatra. It smells exactly like rotten meat. While the **putrid** stench might knock us off our feet, the stinky plant is perfect for attracting beetles and flies that distribute the corpse lily's **pollen**.

As you explore the earth's biomes, you'll discover many other amazing plant and animal adaptations that help them to survive in their biome.

Corpse flower (be glad this isn't a scratch-and-sniff picture!)

ESSENTIAL QUESTION

How does Earth sustain life?

MAKE RECYCLED PAPER

This activity is pretty messy! After you create your own recycled paper, go outside to investigate your home turf in the next activity.

Caution: Have an adult help with the blender.

❯ **Rip scrap paper into teeny pieces.** Place about ½ cup of it into a blender. Pour about 2 cups of hot water over the paper. Repeat this process until the blender is halfway full. Cover the blender and set it at a low speed. Mix the paper and water until it reaches a pulpy consistency. If the blender gets sluggish, add a bit more water.

❯ **Carefully take the pulp outside.** Spread newspaper on a flat surface, and place a towel or rag over it. Set it aside for a moment.

❯ **Place a window screen in a pan or on a baking sheet.** Pour the pulp over the window screen. Wiggle the screen back and forth until the pulp coats it. Gently lift the screen from the pan or sheet, and allow any excess pulp to drip off.

❯ **Set the screen on top of the towel and newspaper.** Keep the screen's pulpy side up. Layer a second towel or rag and more newspaper on top of the screen, creating a sandwich. Use a rolling pin or other tool to press on the sandwich from one end to another until you've wrung out all the water.

❯ **Spread out a third towel or rag in a warm, dry spot**, and carefully place the sandwich on top of it. Allow it to dry for 24 hours. If you live in a humid place, it will probably require more time.

❯ **When the paper is completely dry, peel the newspaper and towels away.** Use this homemade recycled paper in the activity on the next page.

Think About It

How might this method of recycling paper into new paper work for large amounts of paper? Could a factory use this process? What are some ways companies could change this process so they could work with recycled paper from an entire school?

INVESTIGATE YOUR HOME TURF

Activate your senses! Explore the sights, sounds, scents, and textures of a natural environment. Then decorate your homemade recycled paper with treasures you discover on your investigation.

▶ **Go outside and ramble around your home, school, a park, or a natural area.** Drink in the sights and sounds of your environment. Does the scenery include mountains, ravines, prairies, or ponds? What are the weather conditions? What kinds of plant and animal life do you observe?

▶ **Gather a few natural items as you stroll.** Perhaps you'll discover a pinecone or acorn on the ground. Or maybe you'll find a cool leaf or a feather or a pretty flower to press. If you live near the ocean, scout around for a shell. Please don't remove any animals from their habitats, though.

▶ **Decorate the paper you made in the last activity with the little treasures** you harvest from your trek, but leave some space in the middle. Stash the paper away for now. Save it for the last activity in this book.

DID YOU KNOW?

Pet bedding. Bandages. Lampshades. What do these products have in common? All can be made with recycled paper!

Try This!

Go for another ramble in a different part of your town. How are the sights and sounds and smell the same? How are they different? Do you notice any plants and animals?

Chapter 2

DECIDUOUS
FORESTS

Trees, trees, and more trees! These woody wonders define three different forest biomes you'll visit on your worldwide journey. Forests are not only beautiful, they also boast the most **diverse biological** communities in the world. An astonishing variety of plants and animals make their homes in the planet's forests.

ESSENTIAL QUESTION

How are food chains essential to life on Earth?

Forests also provide critical resources for people, including fruits and nuts for food. They supply the wood we use to build homes and furniture and to create pulp and paper products. Forests even provide the essential oxygen we breathe.

WORDS TO KNOW

diverse: a large variety.

biological: having to do with something that is or was living.

17

temperate: climate or weather that is not extreme.

deciduous: plants and trees that shed their leaves each year.

Northern Hemisphere: the half of the planet north of the equator.

fertile: rich in nutrients and good for growing plants.

food chain: a community of animals and plants where each is eaten by another higher up in the chain.

producer: green plants able to make their own food.

photosynthesis: the process plants use to turn sunlight, carbon dioxide, and water into food.

consumer: an organism that eats other organisms.

herbivore: an animal that eats only plants.

omnivore: an animal that eats both plants and animals.

carnivore: an animal that eats only other animals.

food web: a network of connected food chains.

algae: a simple organism found in water that is like a plant but without roots, stems, or leaves.

Let's stop first in the **temperate deciduous** forest. Seasonal changes characterize this biome. A long, warm growing season is followed by a cold winter. Each year, deciduous trees shed their leaves as the weather gets colder.

These forests are one of the earth's most pleasant places, where humans have thrived for thousands of years.

You'll find temperate deciduous forests in the eastern United States, Canada, China, Japan, Russia, and central and eastern Europe. These areas are all in the **Northern Hemisphere**. The soil is **fertile** in these forests, and biodiversity is wide. Every ecosystem contains organisms that interact with one another. One way they intermingle is through feeding patterns.

Trees in a deciduous forest
credit: Watson Media (CC BY 2.0)

FOOD CHAINS AND FOOD WEBS

Which animal feasts on which? **Food chains** illustrate feeding relationships. Let's look at the food chain in the deciduous forest.

Plants are the foundation of the food chain. They are called **producers**, because they make their own food. They do this by capturing the sun's energy in a process called **photosynthesis**. Plants deliver the sun's energy to the animals and people who eat them.

Next in the chain are **consumers**—animals that can't make their own food. Three different kinds of consumers inhabit the deciduous forest. **Herbivores**, such as rabbits, beavers, and grasshoppers, munch only plants. Tasty stems, seeds, grasses, flowers, and fruit provide the nutrition herbivores need. **Omnivores**, such as skunks and wild boars, eat both plants and animals. **Carnivores** eat only the meat of other animals. These hunters include cougars, wolves, and owls.

Food chains illustrate a straight line of what-munches-what. **Food webs** are more complex. For example, a deciduous forest food chain might begin with some **algae**. A prawn eats the algae. A trout then swallows the prawn. And a kingfisher devours the trout. That's a food chain. But kingfishers like to eat frogs, too. Kingfishers and snakes compete for the same food source. Now, the chain has grown into a web.

In any ecosystem, different species not only compete for food but also for sunlight, water, and even mates. Competition is the struggle for resources among different species or among members of the same species.

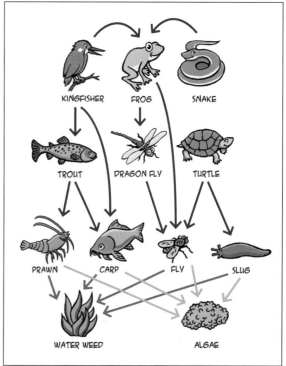

This food chain might be present in a lake or pond.

WORDS TO KNOW

silt: particles of fine soil, rich in nutrients.

component: a part of something.

texture: the feel or consistency of a substance.

nutrients: substances in food and soil that living things need to live and grow.

dense: closely compacted.

decay: to break down and rot.

porous: full of many little holes so water passes through.

aerate: to create channels that allow air to flow through.

horizon: a layer of soil.

topsoil: the top layer of soil.

organic matter: decaying plants and animals.

DIG IT! THE DIRT ON SOIL

Soil in the deciduous forest biome is dark brown and fertile. What's the soil like in your neck of the woods? Depending on where you live or which biome you visit, you'll discover different types. Soil might contain clay, sand, or **silt**. These **components** determine soil's **texture**, or how gritty and clumpy it feels. Why is texture important? In sandy soils, water and **nutrients** drain away rapidly. **Dense** soils are more fertile, but they can become waterlogged.

Soil covers the planet's land surface and is necessary for life.

It might look, well, dirty. But it's full of nutrients, living organisms, and **decaying** organisms. Soil is **porous**, meaning that it's filled with teeny holes or spaces. When rainfall pelts soil, the water flows through all those holes, dissolving nutrients along the way. Thirsty tree and plant roots then slurp up the nutrients.

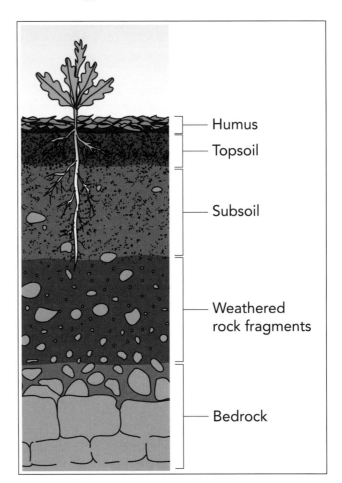

credit: Siyavula Education (CC BY 2.0)

THE LAYERS OF SOIL

Which living organisms of the deciduous forest dig soil? Moles do! With itty-bitty eyes and webbed paws shaped like shovels, they tunnel through the ground and **aerate** soil. Tunnels let air circulate. Burrowing badgers also work the soil, like little striped farmers. Their work creates larger tunnels for rainwater to enter the soil and give thirsty plants a drink.

If you burrowed into soil like a mole on a mission, you'd encounter four layers, or **horizons**. Plants and animals inhabit the ground level, called the **topsoil**. Fertile topsoil is a blend of silt, sand, clay, and **organic matter**. In this layer, seeds sprout and plants take root.

DID YOU KNOW?
Badgers live in burrows called setts. Constructed underground of extensive mazes and tunnels, setts are extremely clean. Badgers refuse to soil them with poop! Instead, at the very edges of their territories, badgers dig special pits to provide toilets for the clan.

Moles dig for their favorite snack, juicy earthworms.

WORDS TO KNOW

leaf litter: fallen leaves and other dead plant material that is starting to break down.

decomposers: bacteria, fungi, and worms that break down wastes and dead plants and animals.

humus: decaying organic matter made from dead plant and animal material.

subsoil: the layer of soil beneath the topsoil.

mineral: a naturally occurring solid found in rocks and in the ground. Rocks are made of minerals. Gold and diamonds are precious minerals.

regolith: a layer of loose rock, also called weathered bedrock.

bedrock: the layer of solid rock under soil.

erosion: the gradual wearing away of rock or soil by water and wind.

polar: the cold climate zones near the North Pole and South Pole.

equator: the imaginary line around the planet halfway between the North and South Poles.

fluctuation: a change.

dormant: when plants are not actively growing during the winter.

Have you ever turned over a clump of topsoil and noticed it's cool to the touch? That's because **leaf litter**, grasses, and other plants protect topsoil from getting too hot and dry. When plants die, insects such as ants, spiders, centipedes, and termites chomp them up into teeny bits.

DID YOU KNOW?

Before gulping a worm, a mole stretches it like a rubber band between clenched paws. Why? To squish yucky grit from its gut!

Decomposers break down waste and dead plants and animals, recycling them into **humus**. Not to be confused with hummus, the delicious dip you slather on pita bread, chocolate-brown-colored humus is organic matter. Rich in nutrients from decomposed plants and animals, humus allows new plants to grow.

The second layer is **subsoil**. **Minerals** and humus mingle together here. You'll also find thirsty roots growing through sticky clay and rocks as they work to locate a water source.

The third layer is **regolith**, or weathered **bedrock**. Weathered means it's been exposed and worn away by weather's activities. In this case, it would have been a long time ago, before all that soil was on top. This deep layer contains no organic matter. Plant roots can't break through this rocky, mineral-filled horizon.

The bottom level is solid bedrock. This unweathered rock hasn't been exposed to the air. However, it might have an opportunity to see daylight someday. An earthquake could blast it to ground level. Or **erosion** could wear away the upper layers.

FOUR DISTINCT SEASONS . . . WITH TREES TO MATCH

A temperate climate experiences a full range of temperatures. Although temperatures may dip to -20 degrees Fahrenheit (-29 degrees Celsius) and peak at close to 100 degrees Fahrenheit (38 degrees Celsius), the average is 50 degrees Fahrenheit (10 degrees Celsius). Yearly rainfall ranges from 29 to 59 inches. During frost-free months, plant life flourishes.

Deciduous forests are nestled between northern **polar** regions and the southern tropics around the **equator**.

Because of the earth's rotation and the sun's slant, temperate deciduous forests enjoy four distinct seasons, each with characteristic weather.

You can learn more about temperate deciduous forests in this video! Do you live in this biome?

PS

🔎 deciduous forests study video

Both frosty Arctic air and warm tropical air whoosh across the zone at different times of the year. These air flows impact the climate.

In temperate climates, snowy winters and hot summers are typically the same length. Yet, even with this dependable pattern, people in temperate zones expect major **fluctuations**. Temperate zoners often say, "Don't like the weather? Just wait a minute and it will change."

In the deciduous forest biome, trees change with the seasons. In winter, trees are **dormant**. During the warm, wet spring, buds bloom with flashy flowers. Broadleaf trees, which bear flowers and fruits, are designed to catch the sun's rays during the summer months. In autumn, these trees shed their leaves in preparation for winter.

WORDS TO KNOW

migrate: to move from one environment to another when seasons change.

hibernate: to spend the winter in a deep sleep.

cache: a collection of things in a place that is hidden or secured.

strata: layers of the forest.

canopy: an umbrella of trees over the forest.

prey: an animal that is killed by another for food.

understory: the second layer of the forest, made up of saplings.

shrub layer: where shrubs and bushes grow in the forest.

herb layer: where berries, herbs, and short bushes grow in the forest.

nectar: a sweet fluid made by flowers that attracts insects.

carpet: the mossy forest floor.

Starlings migrate to warmer climates for the winter months.
credit: Adam (CC BY 2.0)

During autumn, many birds flee the cold and **migrate** to balmier biomes to the south. But not all deciduous forest animals get out of town. Some **hibernate** for the winter. During frozen months, when food is scarce, they settle in for a long winter's nap, snoozing to conserve energy.

Other animals hang around and make some changes to their routines. Without lush greenery to conceal them, animals must adapt to hide from predators.

The least weasel, for example, sprouts a snow-white coat for a winter disguise.

Meanwhile, squirrels pack on an extra 20 percent of their body weight to help them survive the harsh winter. Have you ever stumbled upon a mound of acorns hidden beneath a bush? You probably encountered a secret squirrel stash. Squirrels stow munchies in a **cache**, or food-hiding place, and dip into the hoard throughout the winter.

FOREST STRATA

The deciduous forest has many levels. It's like a high-rise apartment building packed with different residents. The top level earns bragging rights for having the best sunlight. The farther down you roam, the dimmer the light becomes.

The forest is divided into five main layers, or **strata**. On top is the **canopy**. It teems with leafy branches of tall, mature trees that capture as much sunlight as possible. Broadleaf trees, including maples, oaks, and chestnut trees, extend up to 100 feet tall. They shove aside smaller competitors for sunlight and create a cover of shade across the forest like a giant patio umbrella. Great horned owls perch atop trees for a birds-eye view of unsuspecting **prey** on the forest floor.

DID YOU KNOW?

Hummingbirds are airplanes for mites, which are tiny relatives of spiders and ticks. As the hummingbird flits from flower to flower, a teeny, eight-legged mite zips into its nostril to hitch a ride.

Farther down, in some of the lower "apartments," bears doze in cozy nooks.

The second layer is the **understory**, made up of saplings, or young trees. Here, blue jays screech and squirrels somersault from limb to limb like acrobats.

The third layer is the **shrub layer**, which contains shrubs and bushes. It's a key rest stop for chipmunks and other plant-loving animals that munch on crunchy greens and fruits.

Lower down, the **herb layer** features herbs, short plants, and berries. These provide tasty treats for famished raccoons, mice, and voles. Flowers bloom here, attracting bees and hummingbirds with **nectar**.

The fifth layer is the forest floor, or **carpet**. Dark and chilly, the floor is covered with leaf litter. Decomposers such as mushrooms and termites break down decaying leaves and plants and contribute to the biome's fertile soil.

WORDS TO KNOW

transformer: trees that change in winter.

chlorophyll: a pigment that makes plants green, used in photosynthesis to capture light energy.

starch: a white substance found in plant tissues.

stockpile: to store large amounts of something for later use.

bacteria: single-celled organisms found in soil, water, plants, and animals, that decay waste. They are often helpful but sometimes harmful.

fungi: organisms that grow on and feed on rotting things. Plural of fungus.

dung: solid animal waste.

larva: the wormlike stage of an insect's life. The plural is larvae.

Deciduous trees are **transformers**, which means they can change in order to endure bitter winters. During the fall, food production shuts down for the season like an ice cream stand closing up. **Chlorophyll**, a pigment that gives leaves their vivid green hues, breaks down and trees display fall colors until the dead leaves flutter down to join their buddies on the leaf pile.

In winter's chill, trees become dormant. Growth screeches to a halt, and vegetation appears to snooze away the frigid months. Fortunately, trees plan ahead for winter. During the summer months, they turn extra food into **starch** and **stockpile** it for wintry days. Then, when spring fever descends on the biome, trees crank back into food-production mode.

Mushrooms on the forest floor

The Poop on Decomposers

Lowly decomposers tackle a gross job, but somebody's gotta do it. Decomposers even dine on animal waste—poop. **Bacteria**, **fungi**, slugs, and wriggly worms digest and break down dead wood, leaves, plants, insects, and animals. Then, they pass nutrients from decaying carcasses back into the soil. Plants grow by absorbing these nutrients, and the circle of life continues. Covered with copper and metallic green shells, **dung** beetles are attractive decomposers. Dung beetles nestle into fresh animal dung to chow down, make homes, and lay eggs. **Larvae** are worm-like baby beetles. When they hatch, their first meal is ready, all around them!

dung beetle
credit: Frans Van Heerden

CLIMATE CHANGE IN THE WOODS

Climate change sends nature's rhythm out of whack! One way it does this is by shifting the length of the seasons. What happens when there's no long winter's nap? When snow melts too early? It disrupts hibernating species.

Milder, shorter winters throw animals out of sync with their environments. In warmer surroundings, snoozing mammals such as marmots and groundhogs use stored fat too rapidly. They wake up early—and ravenous! With little energy, though, and scarce food available, they often die before scrounging up lunch.

What will the future hold? Scientists predict some animals will adapt to seasonal disruptions, while others will become extinct.

THREATS TO DECIDUOUS FORESTS

Deciduous forests face many threats. Some are natural, such as climate change, disease, forest fires, and insects. And some threats come from humans. For example, during thousands of years, people have chopped down forests for timber or burned them to create farmland.

Some scientists believe **acid rain** is the greatest threat to the deciduous forest. Acid rain is snow or rain that contains deposits of acid. When pollutants from vehicles and factories merge with water droplets in the air, the result is acid rain. This kind of **precipitation** injures leaves and weakens trees. It slows their growth and causes them to produce fewer seeds.

Water Worlds

Do you live near a marsh? A marsh is a type of freshwater wetland commonly found in the deciduous forest biome. Located in low-lying, waterlogged areas, marshes border lakes, ponds, and streams. Plants and animals thrive in marshes. For example, reeds and cattails grow in and around them. Reeds are tall, stalky grasses, while cattails are plants with thick stems, long shoots, and bristly seed heads. Herons and cranes, two types of large birds, also inhabit marshes. Demonstrating adaptation to their environment, they use their long legs to slosh through water and search for food.

A great blue heron in flight

credit Becky Matsubara

Autumn colors
credit: Nicholas A. Tonelli (CC BY 2.0)

The effects of acid rain can be far-reaching. For example, coal power plants in the southern and midwestern United States produce pollution that doesn't just impact those regions. Instead, the pollution moves with the wind to the northeastern United States, where it falls as acid rain.

For this reason, we have the Clean Air Act, which are the laws that help us keep our air clean.

How can you help preserve deciduous forests? Conserve paper, which is made from trees. For instance, don't throw away paper when you make a mistake. Instead, use both sides of a sheet. And don't forget to recycle paper and newspapers.

In the next chapter, we'll take a look at another kind of forest.

ESSENTIAL QUESTION

How are food chains essential to life on Earth?

FOOD CHAIN FLIPBOOK

Get ready to roll! Use plant and animal actors and animate them in a linear sequence of events to show links of a food chain in action.

❯ **Use a pad of paper and a pencil to plan your animation.** Jot down a plant to launch the chain, for example, a fern, a clump of grass, or a bit of moss. Add a plant-loving animal to chomp the green stuff. Perhaps a grasshopper? Now think of an omnivore to pursue the herbivore, and so on. Which mighty predator tops the chain—and ends the action? The longer the chain, the more fun you'll have.

❯ **Count the number of sheets in your pad of paper, and plan an equal number of drawings.** Make sure there are at least 25 sheets. This will zip along action for a spectacular show! Plan a sequence of events to illustrate links in the food chain.

❯ **Sketch the sequence on scratch paper to practice.** Each illustration should be a little bit different from the one before it.

❯ **Draw the sequence on the pad.** Put one image on each sheet and keep it as near the edge of the page as you can. Continue drawing until the action concludes. Color your illustrations with markers. Just make sure to keep colors consistent from one page to the next.

❯ **You're ready to roll!** Hold the flipbook in one hand. With the thumb of your other hand, grip the book, and ruffle the pages from the front to the back.

Try This!

To explore your artistic creativity further, use an app or online resource to create an animation. Create your own animated mini-movie to illustrate a deciduous forest food chain in action.

Chapter 3

CONIFEROUS
FORESTS

LET'S REVIEW FOR THE BIOMES QUIZ. FIRST QUESTION: WHY ARE THEY CALLED CONIFEROUS TREES?

THAT'S AN EASY ONE!

THE NAME COMES FROM LATIN, "CONE," BECAUSE THEY ARE SHAPED LIKE TRAFFIC CONES.

...AND "FEROUS" BECAUSE THEY LOOK KIND OF FURRY.

WELL, THAT'S NOT WHAT THE BOOK SAYS, BUT MAYBE YOU COULD GET SOME CREDIT FOR CREATIVITY.

Let's roll northward into the gorgeous coniferous forest, the largest terrestrial biome on Earth.

Coniferous trees, which don't shed leaves each year, define this biome, also called the **boreal forest**, or **taiga**. At its southern end, the coniferous forest mingles with **evergreens** in deciduous forests. At the northern end, the coniferous forest merges with treeless Arctic tundra.

Let's explore!

DID YOU KNOW?

Conifer comes from the Latin words *conus*, which means "cone," and *ferre*, "to bear."

ESSENTIAL QUESTION

How are living things adapted for life in the coniferous forest?

WORDS TO KNOW

boreal forest: another name for the coniferous forest biome.

taiga: another name for the coniferous forest biome.

evergreen: a tree that keeps its leaves or needles throughout the year.

closed canopy: when the top branches and leaves of a dense group of trees meet to form a ceiling that light has trouble getting through.

open canopy: when the tops of trees are spaced enough to allow sunlight to filter through.

prolonged: continuing for longer than usual.

AN UNBROKEN BAND

Scientists describe the coniferous forest as an unbroken band of trees. Located in the Northern Hemisphere, it encircles parts of Asia, Canada, Europe, Russia, and the United States. It's like a green wreath, 50 million acres in size!

There are two types of coniferous forest—

DID YOU KNOW?

Boreal is a Greek word that means "north." *Taiga* is a Russian word meaning "swampy pine forest." Swampy areas such as marshes and bogs cut through coniferous forests. Lakes do, too.

closed canopy and **open canopy**. In closed-canopy forests, trees grow in close, tight huddles. They shade the mossy carpet below. In open-canopy forests, trees are scattered and amply spaced. Instead of velvety mosses, patchy gray-green lichens sprawl over the forest floor.

Coniferous forest

The coniferous forest is close kin to the deciduous forest, but they do differ in a few ways. While deciduous forests enjoy four distinct seasons, coniferous forests experience speedy summers and lengthy winters. The growing season is a scant three to four months.

Winters linger for six freezing months, with temperatures plunging to as low as -40 degrees Fahrenheit (-40 degrees Celsius). Fleeting summers only get as high as 70 degrees Fahrenheit (21 degrees Celsius). Chilly temperatures result in slow decomposition, so soil tends to be rocky and spongy. It's waterlogged instead of packed with the nutrients found in humus.

ADAPTED FOR LOOONG WINTERS

While deciduous trees shed leaves, conifers bear cones. Cones hold seeds and scaly needles. Many conifers, also called evergreens, remain gloriously green all year round. Cedar, cypress, fir, larch, pine, and spruce trees abound in the coniferous forest. Hardy deciduous trees such as aspen, poplar, and birch squeeze in here and there.

How do conifers adapt to survive **prolonged**, brutal winters?

Deep, dark green coloring helps evergreens capture as much of the sun's light as possible. A waxy coating on needles protects them from drying out in wintry winds.

Evergreens must take advantage of every minute of the brief growing season, so they keep their needles all year. They don't have time to shed needles in fall and then sprout them again in the spring. Instead, when springtime warmth finally arrives and more water becomes available, evergreens are ready to crank up photosynthesis.

Evergreens are pointed and narrow at the top and wide and full at the bottom. Thanks to this cone shape, snow swooshes off an evergreen's bendable branches like a snowboard off a slope. This adaptation means snow is less likely to accumulate and crack branches under weighty loads.

LIFE IN THE CONIFEROUS FOREST

The coniferous forest biome is not very diverse. Fewer species exist here than in deciduous environments.

Climate Change Corner

Wardrobe Change!

Some animals, such as the snowshoe hare, require specific conditions for survival. The hare is dependent on seasonal snow to camouflage and protect it during long winters. With rising temperatures, snow arrives later and spring melt occurs earlier. What happens when the snow cover shrinks? It reveals a brown landscape. Adapted for long winters, though, the hare is out of sync. Its coat doesn't molt back to brown at the same earlier time. That means it doesn't match its surroundings. Glaring white, the hare sticks out against the landscape. Easy pickings for predators on the prowl!

This snowshoe hare is happy there's snow on the ground.

credit: Denali National Park and Preserve (CC BY 2.0)

During the short summer months, vegetation provides plenty to munch on. Woodpeckers, ravens, and hungry herbivores—including elk, muskrats, and snowshoe hares— pluck juicy treats from blackberry bushes. Meanwhile, predators such as endangered Siberian tigers, grizzly bears, rare lynx, and wandering wolves feast on plentiful prey. Peregrine falcons, also endangered, swoop from rocky ledges to snatch dinner off the forest floor.

DID YOU KNOW?

The world's oldest living tree just happens to be a conifer. An unnamed bristlecone pine grows in California's White Mountains and is an amazing 5,000 years old. This tree sprouted as Egypt's ancient pyramids were being built!

When winter blasts in, some animals migrate. For example, the grosbeak, a finch with an extra-large, seed-snapping beak, flies south. Other animals adapt. The snowshoe hare trades its brown summer coat for a white one that blends in with snow. **Camouflaged**, it remains one hop ahead of the lynx. To maneuver in snow, both animals scramble on long legs. Their webbed paws act as built-in snowshoes.

Bristlecone pine
credit: Rick Goldwaser (CC BY 2.0)

PS **Look at this amazing animated map of the Western Hemisphere developed by scientists at the Cornell Lab of Ornithology.** Track the mesmerizing migratory movements of 118 species of birds.

🔎 mesmerizing migration

WORDS TO KNOW

pelt: an animal skin.

overhunting: when an animal is hunted in great numbers, so much that their population falls to low levels. This can cause extinction.

peril: danger.

amber: hard, fossilized resin. Resin is a sticky substance that oozes from trees.

fossil: the remains or traces of ancient life, including plants and animals.

clear-cut logging: a process in which all or almost all the trees in an area are chopped down.

THREATS TO CONIFEROUS FORESTS

Many species that inhabit coniferous forests are furry mammals. Their striking **pelts** and tasty meat have been desirable for centuries. **Overhunting** has placed many of these animal populations in **peril**. For example, sightings of the Siberian tiger are rare today because people hunted them to excess. Scientists believe fewer than 500 Siberian tigers remain in the wild. Musk deer and caribou were also overhunted, and now face reduced populations.

DID YOU KNOW?

Amber, a beautiful golden-orange material used to create jewelry, is made of **fossilized** conifer resin. Some chunks of amber contain spiders, insects, and plants preserved inside.

Clear-cut logging also threatens the coniferous forest. When people clear land for homes, farms, or industry, they sometimes remove nearly every tree. Clear-cut logging wipes out habitats. It also creates soil erosion. When soil erodes, it loses its top layers, which are full of nutrients. Along with those layers, soil loses its ability to grow plants.

Drawn by its natural beauty, many photographers, artists, hikers, and campers visit the coniferous forest biome. Unfortunately, visitors are sometimes careless with campfires, which can lead to dangerous forest fires.

To help coniferous forests thrive, be sure to practice "carry in, carry out" whenever you go hiking. That means you bring everything you need with you and leave nothing behind, so the environment stays as untouched as possible.

In the next chapter, we'll go someplace very different from coniferous forests—rainforests!

ESSENTIAL QUESTION

How are living things adapted for life in the coniferous forest?

EROSION VESSELS

When soil erodes, it loses top layers, which are packed with nutrients. This experiment will show you how vegetation keeps soil from eroding.

Caution: Ask an adult to cut the bottles for you.

❯ **Using three clear, plastic bottles of the same size,** cut away one side of each bottle. Leave the necks intact.

❯ **Fill each vessel with an equal amount of potting soil.** Leave one vessel as it is. Add a layer of dead leaves, bark, and twigs to the second vessel. Plant small houseplants or grass in the third, from end to end.

❯ **Cut the bottom sections off three more clear plastic bottles.** Cut a small hole at each side of the bottoms. Use three pieces of string to make handles for these collection cups. Hang them over the bottle necks.

❯ **Start a scientific method worksheet and predict what will happen as you pour the same amount of water in each.** Will all the vessels produce the same amount of run-off? Will all run-off be the same color? Will all run-off pass out of the soil in the same period of time? Record your predictions.

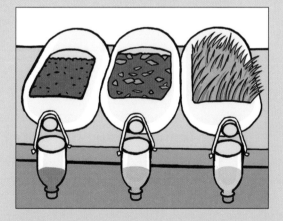

❯ **Pour 1 cup of water into the first erosion vessel.** What happens? Repeat with the others. Measure the run-off that spills into each collection cup.

Think About It

How much soil do you observe in each cup? What does the water look like? Compare and contrast the results. What are your conclusions?

PINE CONE BIRD FEEDER

Go outside and scout around for a plump pine cone. Use the cone's seed case to make a bird feeder and then observe the birds that swoop in for crunchy snacks.

❯ **Place a plate on a flat surface or tabletop** and sprinkle birdseed on it.

❯ **Use a butter knife to spread peanut butter over the pine cone.** Carefully fill in the little nooks and crannies.

❯ **Roll the peanut-buttery cone around in the birdseed** until it's completely covered with seeds.

❯ **Select a prime location for bird watching out your window.** Then tie one end of some string to the top of your pine cone. Tie the other end to a sturdy tree branch.

❯ **Observe birds that visit your feeder. Jot down descriptions in your journal and create sketches.** Use online or print references to identify the feathered friends that flit to your feeder for a snack.

Climate Change Corner

Fire Danger

Climate change alters the very appearance of the planet! This change is evident in high-**latitude** regions such as the boreal forest, which has shrunk. Because of increased fires, deciduous forests have extended their expanse and invaded boreal turf. Hotter and drier conditions create weather events that encourage wildfires. Severe storms bring more frequent lightning strikes, which ignite furious fires. These deadly fires, which can also be caused by human activities, lead to forest loss. This loss causes conifer forests to transform into shrublands.

WORDS TO KNOW

latitude: an imaginary line around the earth that runs parallel to the equator. It measures your position on the earth north or south of the equator.

EXPERIMENT WITH ACID RAIN

Acid rain is a major environmental threat to forest biomes. In coniferous forests, acid rain injures tree needles and hurts their ability to survive frigid winter temperatures. In this experiment, you'll use vinegar, which is an acid, to discover how acid rain affects plant growth.

❯ **Carefully cut away four compartments from an egg carton.** You can recycle the rest of the carton. Use this chart to number the compartments.

❯ **Fill each compartment with potting soil.** Plant beans in each. Prepare four jars with the water and vinegar combinations to correspond with the four egg carton compartments.

Number	Label	Watered with
1	W	Water only
2	5W–1V	Five parts water to one part vinegar
3	1W–1V	One part water to one part vinegar
4	V	Vinegar only

❯ **Start a scientific method worksheet in your science journal and make a chart.** What will happen to the seeds when you water them with each of the liquid combinations? Record your hypothesis for each watering type in one column. Label the other columns "One Week" and "Two Weeks."

❯ **Water the seeds each day with the appropriate liquids.** After one week, note the progress of each compartment in the "One Week" column. Add a small sketch. Repeat after two weeks and update the chart.

❯ **Compare and contrast the plants yielded by the seeds.** What effects do different levels of acid have? What conclusions can you draw about the effects of acid rain on plants?

Think About It

Acid rain doesn't only impact plant growth. On our interconnected planet, it also impacts aquatic ecosystems such as wetlands, lakes, and streams. How might toxic chemicals in water harm fish and shellfish? How could impacted aquatic wildlife enter other food chains?

Chapter 4

TROPICAL
RAINFORESTS

Let's journey south to the world's rainiest biome, the tropical rainforest. Although rainforests cover only 7 percent of Earth's land surface, half of the planet's animal and plant species make their homes here.

Tropical rainforests are located near the equator, between the **Tropic of Cancer** and the **Tropic of Capricorn**. Go back to the map on page 5 to see where these are. You'll find tropical rainforests in Australia, Central and South America, the Pacific Islands, Southeast Asia, and West Africa. Tropical rainforests experience little fluctuation in temperature. Frost never develops in this moist, hot biome, and plants never become dormant. Average rainfall is 80 to 160 inches, while the average temperature is 80 degrees Fahrenheit (27 degrees Celsius).

ESSENTIAL QUESTION

Why are tropical rainforests called "the lungs of the planet?"

LIVING IN LEVELS

As with its deciduous cousin, the tropical rainforest is multi-leveled with different flora and fauna at each layer. The top level is the **emergent layer**, where mushroom-shaped treetops burst out of the forest. Huge broadleaf trees tower 250 feet in the air.

These green giants support their own weight as well as the load of all the critters that live in them. How do they pull this off in the rainforest's shallow, soggy soil? With thick, aboveground roots called **buttresses**. These massive, woody feet fan out around the base of each tree as natural supports.

WORDS TO KNOW

tropical rainforest: a biome where it is warm all the time.

Tropic of Cancer: a line of latitude north of the equator, marking the northernmost point at which the sun can appear directly overhead at noon.

Tropic of Capricorn: a line of latitude south of the equator, marking the southernmost point at which the sun can appear directly overhead at noon.

emergent layer: the top level of trees, which get the most sun, above the canopy.

buttresses: thick, aboveground roots that support tall trees.

The emergent layer is home to bats, butterflies, harpy eagles, howler monkeys, and snakes. What's the benefit of living up there? That's where the most sunlight is. On the flip side, though, it's pummeled with fierce winds and torrential rains. The top level also endures incredible heat.

WORDS TO KNOW

liana: a woody vine that wraps itself around the trunks and branches of trees in an effort to reach the sunlight.

In this hot, moist environment, bacteria and fungi grow fast, so decomposition is speedy. It's important that healthy plants shed water quickly so they don't decay.

Leaves are adapted with pointy tips that let rainwater run off quickly.

The next level down is the canopy, shaped like an open umbrella. Here, broadleaf trees stretch toward the sun, as high as 90 feet. Most rainforest animals hang out in this bustling and colorful level, where sunlight—and noise—is abundant. Colorful toucan birds munch on tasty leaves, fruits, and nuts. Sluggish sloths hang upside down by hooking tree limbs with curved claws. Hummingbirds, including those that migrated from deciduous forests for the winter, slip needle-nose bills into flowers to sip sweet nectar.

Let's move down. What's the best way to travel here? Fly, glide, leap, and swing! Snag a sturdy vine to swoop through the understory. Smaller trees and shrubs compete for space in this cooler, damp layer, where sunlight is limited.

A red howler monkey in the rainforest.

credit: Jason Rothmeyer (CC BY 2.0)

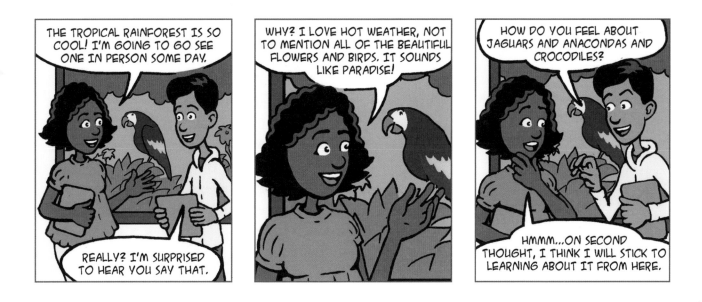

Plants grow gigantic leaves here, an adaptation that allows them to capture as much of the sun's energy as possible. Patchy lichens, ferns, and delicate orchids grow in this level. Insects, such as spiders, walking sticks, beetles, bees, and army ants, also live here.

At the bottom level sprawls the forest floor. Little sunlight penetrates down here. Carnivorous predators, including agile jaguars and bone-crushing anacondas, stalk this dark level. Seeds, fruits, and branches fall to the ground, where herbivores devour them before they decay in the tropical heat. Unlike the rich soil of temperate deciduous forests, rainforest soil is low in nutrients. Pounding rains flush them away.

Lianas, which are lanky, woody vines, hang throughout the rainforest. Lianas begin life as seeds scattered on the forest floor. As lianas grow, they drape themselves around trees and climb high to soak in the sun's rays.

DID YOU KNOW?

Coconut, an important food in the tropics, is the fruit of the coco palm. It is considered one of the world's most useful trees. People use the coco palm's leaves to make thatched roofs, umbrellas, baskets, and fans. They carve coconut shells into beautiful bowls, cups, and ladles, as well as buttons for shirts and sweaters.

greenhouse gas: a gas that traps heat in the earth's atmosphere and contributes to the greenhouse effect and global warming.

global warming: an increase in the average temperature of the earth's atmosphere, enough to cause climate change.

deforestation: the process through which forests are cleared to use land for other purposes.

prehensile: able to grasp things.

THREATS TO RAINFORESTS

Scientists have nicknamed rainforests "the lungs of the planet." Abundant plant life in the rainforest provides 20 percent of the world's oxygen. It also cleans the air of carbon dioxide, a major **greenhouse gas**. Through the process of photosynthesis, plants use energy from sunlight, water from soil, and carbon dioxide from air to make their own food—and they also release oxygen.

DID YOU KNOW?

Many canopy animals never descend to the forest floor. They stay high in the canopy their whole lives.

This job of removing carbon dioxide from the atmosphere is important.

When too much greenhouse gas is in the air, more of the sun's heat is trapped on Earth, contributing to **global warming**. The planet needs just the right amount of greenhouse gases in the air to maintain the right temperature.

Earth's lungs are shrinking—fast. **Deforestation**, occurring at an alarming rate, threatens the rainforest biome. People clear land for mining and farming and to build homes. As they do, they destroy habitats for thousands of precious species, including those that can't be found anywhere else on the planet. In fact, some scientists believe that about 35 rainforest species become extinct each day through deforestation.

What's your carbon footprint?
That's the amount of greenhouse gases you produce to support your activities. Calculate your footprint—and then make an action plan to reduce it!

PS

🔍 Nature carbon calculator

MORE AMAZING ANIMAL ADAPTATIONS

Meet the okapi, nicknamed the "forest giraffe." This rare animal is native to Central Africa's Ituri Forest. With striped forelegs and hindquarters, it resembles a zebra. Yet the okapi's long, **prehensile** tongue—adapted for grasping and yanking tasty leaves—provides a clue that it's related to the giraffe. Why doesn't the okapi have a giraffe's long neck and stilt-like legs? It must dodge dangling lianas and chunky buttresses to forage for food. Lanky limbs and a stretchy neck would just get in the way!

Speaking of tongues, don't forget Australia's echidna. This small, spiky mammal forages across the forest floor, thrusting a snuffling snout into termite nests or anthills. It shoves a spiky tongue, coated with sticky saliva, inside. Nutritious insects get trapped on the gooey coating. The echidna reels in its tongue and smooshes bugs into pulp in its toothless mouth.

Now that you've wandered the lush rainforest, let's go to someplace where there's plenty of sunshine for everyone at every level—the desert!

ESSENTIAL QUESTION

Why are tropical rainforests called "the lungs of the planet?"

Climate Change Corner

NASA Time-Lapse

Watch NASA's time-lapse animation, which shows satellite images of deforestation in the Amazon rainforest. The animation depicts the years 1975 through 2011.

PS How has deforestation, a human activity, changed the surface of the Earth? What do you observe about the intensifying rate of deforestation? What conclusions do you draw?

🔍 time lapse deforestation amazon

PLANT YOUR OWN HUMMINGBIRD GARDEN

Hummingbirds don't have a sense of smell. Instead, they respond to color, especially large groups of flowers in reds, pinks, and oranges. Let's plant a colorful garden and invite the world's smallest bird to visit!

Hummingbird

With teeny needle-nose bills, hummingbirds prefer trumpet-shaped flowers with slim, long necks. They especially love flowers oozing with nectar, their top food source. Do some research before you plant your garden. Find out which species of hummingbirds live in your area. Learn about the kinds of flowers that attract hummingbirds. Investigate which flowers will thrive in your location and won't be **invasive species**.

❯ **Locate a space for your garden and choose flowers and shrubs suitable for your region.** A suggested list is included.

❯ **Plan for your garden in your science journal.** Divide the flowerbed into sections, and label where you will plant each item. Read planting directions, so you'll know how much space to leave between each plant.

❯ **Wear gardening gloves and use a shovel to dig holes in soil.** While you're at it, take a close look at the soil. Is there enough humus to help the plants grow? If not, you may have to add a bit of **compost**. Can you find bits of sand, clay, or gravel? How about wriggly worms and roly-poly bugs?

WORDS TO KNOW

invasive species: a species that is not native to an ecosystem and rapidly expands to crowd out other species.

compost: decayed food scraps and vegetation that can be put back in the soil.

▶ **Following your plan, place each plant in soil, and refill the hole.** Pat the soil back into place. Thoroughly water the garden daily with a garden hose. If you're lucky, a hummingbird might flit into the mist for a quick spritz! Hummingbirds enjoy misty sprays. Stick broken branches into the garden here and there to make perches for hummingbirds.

▶ **Find a safe perch nearby, such as a tree limb, away from predators.** Ask an adult to help you punch a small hole into a bucket. Tear off a bit of a rag to stop up the hole. Then pour a small amount of water into the bucket, and hang it from the perch.

▶ **Fill a birdbath with fresh water and place it beneath the bucket.** Now, you have a dripping shower, where hummingbirds can hover to grab quick splatters. Provide fresh water daily.

DID YOU KNOW?

When Spanish explorers encountered vibrant hummingbirds in the New World, they called them *joyas volardores*, or "flying jewels." It's an ideal description for the shimmery birds, which can flap their wings an average of 50 times per second!

Think About It

Observe the hummingbirds that visit your garden. In your journal, add sketches and notes to those that you made for your Pine Cone Bird Feeder. What differences and similarities do you observe?

Suggested Flower Choices

* bee balm
* bleeding heart
* bougainvillea
* coral bells
* coral honeysuckle
* fuchsia
* hollyhock
* impatiens
* Indian paintbrush
* petunia
* red columbine
* trumpet vine

Suggested Shrub Choices

* agastache
* azalea
* butterfly bush
* gooseberry
* lilac
* red-flowering currant
* Rose of Sharon
* thimbleberry

RAINFOREST CRUNCH 'N' MUNCH

Try this for a crunchy rainforest snack! Add some ingredients that come from rainforests to make this sweet and crispy no-cook snack. This recipe makes 22 quarter-cup servings.

Ingredients

1 cup rice cereal	½ cup Brazil nuts	¼ cup shredded coconut
1 cup corn cereal	½ cup cashews	
1 cup dried banana chips	¼ cup semi-sweet chocolate bits	½ teaspoon ground cinnamon
1 cup dried pineapple		

▶ **Measure and pour cereals, banana chips, pineapple, and nuts into a mixing bowl.** Gently stir the mixture with a wooden spoon. Sprinkle chocolate bits, shredded coconut, and cinnamon over the top.

▶ **Serve with a spoon.** Store the remaining mixture in a tightly sealed container for up to three days.

Climate Change Corner

Save the Chocolate!

Hot fudge sundaes. Devil's food cake. Mole sauce. What do these sweet and savory foods have in common? Chocolate or cocoa powder! Around the world, chocolate is a favorite food. It's a high-demand product, which means many people want to buy it. Climate change will impact its future. Why? Chocolate is made from the seeds, or cocoa beans, of the evergreen cacao tree. To thrive, cacao trees require soil rich in nitrogen, high humidity, plentiful rain, and consistent temperatures. NOAA, the National Oceanic and Atmospheric Administration, tells us, "Chocolate grows best in the places where it would quickly melt in your hands." What happens as those places become warmer and drier? They lose moisture retained in soil. Soil becomes less hospitable to cacao **cultivation**. In response to challenges, cacao growers are working to selectively breed seeds that are drought-resistant. Now, that's a sweet adaptation!

WORDS TO KNOW

cultivation: preparing and using land to grow crops.

DESERTS

You were drenched by torrential rains in Earth's wettest biome, the tropical rainforest. Now, let's dry off in its most arid biome—the desert. In some deserts, blisteringly hot days transform into shivery nights and parched landscapes explode into vibrant life when infrequent rainstorms sweep in.

ESSENTIAL QUESTION

What changes will occur if the desert continues to be Earth's fastest growing biome?

About 20 percent of the planet's surface is comprised of deserts—and that percentage continues to grow. You'll find deserts in Australia, India, Israel, Iran, Iraq, and Mexico. They're also located in Africa and in the southwestern United States.

WORDS TO KNOW

arid: very dry, receiving little rain.

parched: dried out.

coarse: composed of large particles.

pleated: folded.

transpiration: the evaporation of water from plants, usually through tiny pores in their leaves called stomata.

taproot: a root that grows down vertically to make contact with water deep underground.

Extremely low levels of rainfall characterize the desert, where daily temperatures can careen from a scorching 110 degrees Fahrenheit (37 degrees Celsius) during the day to a frigid 30 degrees Fahrenheit (-1 degree Celsius) at night.

Why do temperatures nose-dive so drastically? Desert air is extremely dry. Because the air contains scant moisture, it's not able to cling to much heat. When the sun sets, temperatures plummet.

DID YOU KNOW?

What's the hottest temperature ever recorded? Death Valley, in California, scored that scorching honor when the thermometer soared to 134 degrees Fahrenheit (56.7 degrees Celsius) in 1913.

The Thar Desert in India
credit: sushmita balasubramani (CC BY 2.0)

DESERT ADAPTATIONS

In the extreme environment of the desert, survival is tricky. Soil is **coarse**, rocky, and salty. Plants encounter frequent droughts. The bristly Saguaro cactus has adapted to these harsh conditions by developing stems **pleated** like accordions. When rain makes a rare appearance, the pleats puff up. They suck in water, stash it away, and tap into the supply during droughts.

The Saguaro also has a waxy coating on its skin, which seals in moisture and cuts down on transpiration.

Meanwhile, Joshua trees use spiky, hairy leaves to protect themselves from fierce winds and sun. These "trees" are actually members of the lily family, and can grow as high as 40 feet! You'll only find them in the Mojave Desert of Arizona, California, Nevada, and Utah.

Saguaro cactus
credit: SonoranDesertNPS (CC BY 2.0)

In South Australia, the crimson Sturt's desert pea survives by using a **taproot**. The vertical taproot plunges straight down, seeking out water from deep in the ground.

WORDS TO KNOW

nocturnal: describes an animal that is active at night instead of during the day.

burrows: underground holes and tunnels where animals live.

radiate: to spread outward.

oxymoron: a figure of speech that seems contradictory.

ADAPTED FOR THE DESERT

How do animals survive in the dry, challenging environment of the desert? Most avoid the sun's heat by hanging out in shady areas around rocks and under shrubs, such as the creosote bush. Many animals are **nocturnal**—they scout for food only at night. During hot days, they hide under sand in cool **burrows**.

Most desert mammals are small. Big guys haven't adapted for life in this harsh biome.

What do the bilby from Australia, the jackrabbit of the American Southwest, and the fennec fox of Africa have in common? All these pint-sized creatures have jumbo ears! Big ears **radiate** heat, allowing it to escape from the animals' bodies so they can keep cool. The fennec fox also sports thick fur on its feet to protect them against the desert's broiling hot sands.

A fennec fox
credit: Tim Parkinson (CC BY 2.0)

Meanwhile, the leopard gecko, found in Iran, Iraq, and Pakistan, relies on super-thick skin to keep from shriveling up like a prune in the dry desert. This insect eater uses a plump tail to store fat when food is scarce. But that's not all it does. When a ravenous predator, such as a fox or snake, grabs the gecko's tail, part of it comes off! This momentarily baffles the predator, giving the gecko an opportunity to scurry off. Later, the lost segment grows back.

DID YOU KNOW?

Like other members of the cuckoo family of birds, roadrunners have two toes that face forward and two that point backward. Perfect for dashing over sand to catch prey!

The roadrunner gets water from its food. You'll find roadrunners in the Chihuahuan, Mojave, Sonoran, and southern Great Basin Deserts, all located in North America. These speedy birds, members of the cuckoo family, zoom at 15 miles per hour. They eat scorpions, lizards, and even deadly rattlesnakes.

A Cold Desert?

A cold desert sounds like an **oxymoron** because most people associate deserts with heat. Deserts aren't only about camels and tumbleweeds. Antarctica is the planet's coldest, driest, most blustery place. You wouldn't expect it to be a desert, but it is. It's a cold desert swathed in a permanent ice sheet that reaches a depth of 15,669 feet. Antarctica receives nearly the same amount of moisture each year as the Sahara Desert! How cold can a desert get? One unforgettably frigid July day in 1983, the temperature plunged to a bone-rattling -129 degrees Fahrenheit (-89 degrees Celsius) in Vostok, Antarctica.

THREATS TO DESERTS

Because of human activity and climate change, the desert is the earth's quickest growing biome. **Desertification**, which turns fertile land into dry land, occurs in other biomes and creates more deserts. Desertification can happen when people clear land for crops. By doing so, they remove vegetation that protects soil from erosion.

Ranching also threatens other biomes, including tropical rainforests, and can turn them into deserts. When plant-munching animals **overgraze**, all the plants are gobbled up. What's more, the hooves of **grazing** animals stir up fragile soil and cause it to wear away.

Cactus collection threatens the desert, too. Visitors to the biome, thrilled by beautiful and exotic cacti, yank them out of sandy soil and sneak them home. It's against the law, and it often results in dead plants and dwindling species. Never take a cactus—or any plant—from its environment.

Now that we've explored some of the hottest and coldest places on Earth, let's make our way to a biome that's either temperate or tropical—the grasslands!

ESSENTIAL QUESTION

What changes will occur if the desert continues to be Earth's fastest growing biome?

Pictograph

A **pictograph** is a symbol used to represent a word or an idea. For example, the symbol of a lightning bolt might stand for the word lightning. To tell stories, ancient people created pictographs on rock surfaces. Modern people have discovered pictographs all over the world, including in deserts in the American Southwest.

Pictographs in Utah desert made by early humans
credit: Thomas (CC BY 2.0)

PAINT YOUR OWN PICTOGRAPHS

One of the most common pictographs is the human handprint. Through art, ancient people also honored the sun, moon, and stars. For pigment, they combined animal fat with berries, blood, charcoal, clay, and minerals such as chalk. Create your own chalk pigments to paint rock pictographs!

❯ **Go outside and scout around for interesting rocks of various sizes.** Wide, flat rocks work well, but bumpy or grooved rocks are great, too. Choose a few small ones for the activity on page 57. Set them aside as you make your own paint.

❯ **Spread newspaper over your work area.** Slip a sealable bag inside another. Place a piece of chalk in the inside bag and firmly seal both bags. Use a rubber mallet or other tool to smash the chalk to a fine powder.

DID YOU KNOW?

Native Americans used the Joshua tree's sturdy leaves to weave baskets and shoes.

❯ **Pour the powder into a small plastic tub.** Add a bit of water. Use a craft stick to blend the powder and water until it's smooth.

❯ **Add white glue to the mixture and blend.** Slowly add water to achieve a smooth consistency. You will most likely need about 2 or 3 tablespoons of water.

❯ **Use corn husks, twigs, feathers, and your fingertips—all methods ancient people used—to paint pictographs on the rocks.** You can research ancient pictographs for inspiration.

Try This!

Repeat with chalks of other colors or try blending chalks to make new colors! Can you devise symbols of your own for people, animals, events, and activities that are important in your life?

MAKE YOUR OWN RAINSTICK

It is unknown where rainsticks originated. Some people think the first version of a rainstick was called a tubular rattle and was made out of reeds by indigenous peoples in South American and Africa.

❯ **A long tube makes the best rain sounds, so use a wrapping paper or postal tube.** Trace the end of the tube onto a flat piece of cardboard. Repeat, so that you have two cardboard circles. Cut out the circles. These are the end plugs for your rainstick. Use glue to attach one end plug. Reinforce it with masking tape.

❯ **Measure a sheet of foil so that it's twice as long as your tube.** Firmly roll the foil into a long, spiraling coil about ½-inch thick. Press the coiled foil into your tube. This is the rainstick's sound filter.

❯ **Pour a combination of rice, lentils, beans, popcorn kernels, or other products** into a measuring cup until you have about ½ cup. Slip a funnel into the open end of the tube, and pour the mixture inside. It will produce your rain sound.

❯ **Conduct a sound test.** Use your palm to plug the open end and let the ingredients run from one end of the tube to the other. Is it music to your ears? You might want to add a bit more of the dried products. But don't make the rainstick too heavy, or it will be cumbersome to play.

❯ **With glue and masking tape, attach the second end plug.** Use paints to decorate the rainstick with desert plants and critters.

DID YOU KNOW?

The Atacama Desert of Chile and Peru is the world's driest place. How dry is it? Not even cacti grow there! The parched Atacama usually receives only 1 inch of rain each year.

Try This!

Don't stop there! Compose a rainstick rhythm and perform it.

WORDS TO KNOW

indigenous peoples: people who first inhabited a region.

MAKE A DESERTARIUM

Have you ever planted a terrarium in a jar? Give your green thumb some exercise by building a desertarium, or a miniature desert!

❱ **Wearing gardening gloves, line the bottom of a large, clear glass container** with a ½-inch layer of crushed charcoal. Charcoal soaks up odors and keeps soil from becoming stinky. Cover with a 1-inch layer of gravel or pebbles.

❱ **Combine two parts potting soil, one part sand, and one part compost.** Spread at least 2 inches of this mixture over the gravel or pebbles. You'll probably notice the soil is a bit moist from the compost. Make sure it's only damp and not wet when you add the plants. When conditions are too wet, fungus can grow.

❱ **Plan an artistic landscape for your plants.** With a garden shovel and your hands, form mounds and valleys in the soil.

❱ **Now add plants.** Buy some **succulents** at a local gardening store and position the plants artistically in the mounds and valleys. Handle cacti with care so the prickles don't pop through your gloves! Decorate the desert landscape with your pictograph rocks from page 55.

❱ **Place the desertarium in a sunny location.** Cacti and succulents are relatively slow-growing plants. You won't need to closely tend them, but check from time to time to make sure they're thriving. Always leave your desertarium uncovered. That way, moisture will evaporate and conditions will remain dry as a bone.

Think About It

How are the conditions in your desertarium different from those in a terrarium? How would your succulents do in a terrarium?

WORDS TO KNOW

terrarium: a small enclosed habitat.

desertarium: a small, enclosed desert habitat.

succulents: plants with thick, fleshy leaves and stems that can store water.

57

Chapter 6

TEMPERATE
GRASSLANDS

Take a stroll through Earth's **grasslands**. This biome covers approximately 20 percent of the planet, and can be found on every continent except Antarctica. Grasslands are usually located in the middle of continents, sandwiched between deserts and forests. Like forests, grasslands can be either temperate or tropical, depending on location.

Let's investigate temperate grasslands first. Grasslands are treeless, wide-open spaces north of the Tropic of Cancer and south of the Tropic of Capricorn. Depending on where they're located, grasslands are referred to by many different names. Grasslands sprawl over Canada's **prairies** and across the United States' **plains**. They stretch through South America's **pampas**, over **Eurasia's steppes**, and across South Africa's **veldts**.

ESSENTIAL QUESTION

How are grasses and hooved animals adapted to thrive in wide-open spaces?

Temperate grasslands experience a wide variety of temperatures. Depending on the season, the thermometer might dip to −40 degrees Fahrenheit (−40 degrees Celsius) or climb to 100 degrees Fahrenheit (38 degrees Celsius).

Winters are cold and dry and springs are wet with rain. Soil here is rich, but biodiversity is lower than in the tropical savannas you'll visit in the next chapter.

WORDS TO KNOW

grassland: a large area of land covered with grass.

prairie: a term for a temperate grassland, primarily used in Canada, but also in the United States.

plains: a term for a temperate grassland, primarily used in the United States, but also in Canada.

pampas: a term for a temperate grassland in South America, especially Argentina.

Eurasia: the land mass of Europe and Asia.

steppe: a term for a temperate grassland in Russia and the Ukraine.

veldt: a term for a temperate grassland in South Africa.

Illinois prairie sky

AMBER WAVES OF GRAIN

Unlike forests, where trees are **dominant**, grasslands are full of grasses, such as barley, buffalo grass, coneflowers, oats, pampas grass, and wheat. When wind blows over the plains of the American Midwest, for example, you'll see waves of grain fluttering over huge, flat expanses of land.

Soil here is bursting with nutrients. It's ideal for growing corn, oats, and wheat. These crops are used to produce breads and cereals for the entire country.

No wonder this part of the country is nicknamed the "Nation's Breadbasket."

Howling coyote
credit: USFWS Mountain-Prairie (CC BY 2.0)

Animals have plenty to eat here, too. Large grazing herbivores and many insect species thrive in grasslands. For example, you can find bison, elk, pronghorn, wild burros, and wild horses rambling over North America's plains. You can also find carnivores such as coyotes, foxes, snakes, and wolves.

DID YOU KNOW?

The United States is the tornado capital of the world. In an average year, about 1,253 tornadoes twist through the country.

ADAPTED FOR WIDE, OPEN SPACES

Grasses are well adapted to the blustery environment of wide-open spaces. With **supple** stems, grasses easily bow when windy gusts sweep over them. Built to endure drought, grass leaves are slender to prevent water loss.

The roots of grasses extend deep into the dark soil, seeking out water. Deep roots also prevent the grasses from being completely yanked out by hungry herbivores. And when wildfires burn grasses aboveground, the deep, hardy roots survive below. They launch sprouts out of the ground to start regrowth.

Ungulates are mammals with hooves, such as antelope, bison, and horses. Hooves are adaptations for tromping through tall grasses. Did you know a hoof is actually an oversized toenail? It's a thorny and scaly **sheath** that protects the foot. Scientists believe early grassland animals walked on their toes and developed long legs so they could outrun predators.

Wild Horses

In many grasslands, wild horses are beloved symbols of the prairies. Many people believe wild horses should be protected as native wildlife. Others, including cattle ranchers worried about their herds, consider them an invasive species. But are wild horses really alien invaders? Some scientists dispute the claim. Fossils show that horse lineages probably originated in North America about 4 million years ago. These creatures traveled to other continents before going extinct in North American about 12,000 years ago. Years later, in the 1500s, Spanish explorers journeyed to North America. They brought domesticated horses—descendants of North American *Equus* travelers—to the continent and reintroduced them to ecosystems. The wild horses that roam our prairies today are descendants of those long-ago wanderers. What do you think? Invasive or native?

Life in wide-open spaces is full of peril. Unlike creatures in forest biomes, grassland animals can't climb trees to escape predators. How have they adapted? Prairie dogs, native to North America, spend much of their time digging extensive burrows.

When predators such as bobcats or badgers slink up, the prairie dog dashes below ground to safety.

Say What?

Chatter. Chirps. Chees. The language of prairie dogs! They communicate with one another in interconnected burrows underground and in villages aboveground. Their chatter is far more complex than once believed. Professor Con Slobodchikoff of Northern Arizona University spent more than 30 years studying the ways the rodents "talk" to one another. Through recordings and tests, he discovered they employ different tones to sound the alarm for a variety of predators, from hawks overhead to coyotes on the prowl and even to people and their dogs sniffing around.

Kissing prairie dogs
credit: USFWS Mountain-Prairie (CC BY 2.0)

(PS) You can listen to Professor Slobodchikoff talk about his work and hear some prairie dog conversations at this website.

🔍 animal cognition prairie dog

Another burrowing grassland animal is the endangered pink fairy armadillo from Argentina. Its favorite food? Ants! It builds burrows next to anthills.

The pink fairy armadillo
credit: Cliff (CC BY 2.0)

The pink fairy armadillo is named for its delicate rose coloring. It's only 4 inches long, making it the smallest member of the armadillo family. With sharp claws, armor plates, and a stout tail, the pink fairy armadillo is an expert digger. Once it tunnels through the earth, it uses its hind plate and tail to block the burrow opening.

DID YOU KNOW?

The pink fairy armadillo produces sounds like a wailing baby!

THREATS TO GRASSLANDS

Natural wildfires are one of the biggest threats to grasslands. But humans cause problems, too. Because grasslands are flat and fertile, they're perfect for farming and grazing. Both activities deplete the biome, especially when grazing is excessive. And when people plow too much during the dry season, they make land vulnerable to dust storms.

Have you heard of the Dust Bowl? It happened during the 1930s. This was when farmers spent years plowing up too much topsoil in the plains, and then a long drought took hold of the region. Dust storms happened frequently and people suffered an economic disaster as well as an environmental one.

Now let's journey to the cousin biome of temperate grasslands—tropical grasslands!

ESSENTIAL QUESTION

How are grasses and hooved animals adapted to thrive in wide-open spaces?

TORNADO IN A BOTTLE

Do you live in Tornado Alley? That's the nickname of the central Great Plains region of the United States. Its geography is ripe for tornado activity. South of the Great Plains lie the deserts of the Southwest, where hot, dry air forms. The Gulf of Mexico, where warm, humid air masses develop, is to the southeast. In the Rocky Mountains to the west, cold, dry air forms.

April, May, and June are peak tornado months. During that time, warm, humid air becomes trapped beneath hot, dry air and cold, dry air and the pressure builds. When warm, humid air finally blasts free, it causes explosive thunderstorms. A twister twirls through the sky and touches ground, causing great destruction. You can make your own tornado in a bottle and watch a **vortex** develop.

❯ **Use two empty, 2-liter bottles.** Pour water into one bottle until it's about two-thirds full. Add three squirts of dish detergent. Then, add three drops of food coloring. Add a dash of glitter, sequins, or tiny beads to represent items from the ground that get sucked up into the vortex.

❯ **Place a flat metal washer on top of the filled bottle.** Turn the empty plastic bottle upside down. Place it on top of the washer so the two bottles are connected, with the empty bottle on top. Use duct tape to tightly join the bottles.

❯ **Turn over the connected bottles so the full bottle is on top.** Place the bottles on a steady flat surface or table. What do you notice? Holding both bottles, swirl them in a **clockwise** circle. Do you see water rotating in the top bottle? Does a funnel shape develop when the top bottle drains more rapidly? That's the vortex.

Think About It

How does the vortex form? As you rotate the water, **centripetal forces** draw it toward the center of the bottle. Gravity tugs the water to the drain hole. These two actions occur at the same time. When water drains into the bottom bottle, the vortex develops.

WORDS TO KNOW

vortex: a rapidly whirling spiral of air or water.

clockwise: the direction that follows the hands of a clock.

centripetal forces: forces that pull a moving object toward a center area.

SALT AND SEED GERMINATION

During periods of drought, soil becomes salty. How does salt concentration in soil impact seed germination? Sprout radish seeds to find out!

❯ **Use three plastic deli tubs of the same size.** Individually label the tubs, each with a different solution identifier: Solution 1: 1 Teaspoon; Solution 2: 2 Teaspoons; Solution 3: 3 Teaspoons.

❯ **Place a piece of paper towel or coffee filter at the bottom of each container.** Sprinkle quick-sprouting radish seeds over each piece. Label three plastic cups to match the solution identifiers of each deli tub.

❯ **Prepare the solutions.** Pour 1 cup of distilled water into each plastic cup. In the Solution 1 cup, add 1 teaspoon of salt. In the Solution 2 cup, add 2 teaspoons. In the Solution 3 cup, add 3 teaspoons. Stir to thoroughly dissolve the salt.

❯ **Use an eyedropper to add a small amount of each solution to its corresponding container.** Make sure you completely wet each paper towel or coffee filter, but don't drench it. Cover each container with a piece of clingwrap.

❯ **Start a scientific method worksheet and predict what will happen over a two-week period as you tend the seeds.** How will different salt solutions impact seed germination? How will the solutions affect seedlings as they begin to grow?

❯ **Place the containers in the same location, where they can receive sunlight undisturbed.** Monitor the seeds each day. Write down your observations. Add more solution to each corresponding plant. After two weeks, assess and analyze your results. What are your findings about soil content's impact on germination and growth?

Think About It

What do your conclusions mean for large-scale agriculture? What happens when entire farms have soil that becomes too salty?

SSS-SOFT PRETZEL SSS-SNAKES

With no limbs and elongated bodies, snakes are able to slither through dense grasses and into burrows to catch prey. They can also move quickly to escape predators. Their coloring allows them to blend in with grassy surroundings. Try some of your own snakes as a snack! Makes approximately 12 snakes.

Caution: Have an adult help with the stove.

Ingredients

2 teaspoons instant yeast
2 cups water at room temperature
3 cups white whole wheat flour
2 tablespoons sugar
1 tablespoon salt
food coloring (optional)

2½ to 3 cups unbleached all-purpose flour
6 cups water
2 tablespoons baking soda
egg glaze: 1 egg combined with
    1 tablespoon water
sesame seeds or coarse salt
mustard (optional)

❯ **For this project, you may want to start by researching different species of grassland snakes, such as a Butler's garter snake, smooth green snake, brown snake, and fox snake.** Study photos of the reptiles in their habitats. Then, use pictures as a springboard for your creativity as you follow the recipe and design your own snake pretzels!

❯ **In a large mixing bowl, combine the yeast, 2 cups water, white whole wheat flour, sugar, and salt.** If you'd like to color your snake, add a few drops of food coloring. Slowly add some unbleached flour and mix until you have a soft dough. The dough should not be sticky.

❯ **Remove the dough from the bowl and place it on a floured board.** Knead the dough thoroughly. Then, place it back in the bowl, cover, and allow it to rise until doubled in size.

❯ **Once the dough has doubled, divide it into 12 pieces of approximately the same size.** Roll each piece between your fingers to form a snake.

❯ **Measure 6 cups of water into a large pot.** Add baking soda and bring the water to a boil. In the meantime, coat a baking sheet with non-stick spray and preheat the oven to 450 degrees Fahrenheit (230 degrees Celsius).

❯ **When the water boils, place four snakes at a time into the pot.** Allow them to boil for 1 minute. Then, carefully remove them with a slotted spoon and place them on a cooking sheet.

❯ **After you have boiled all the snakes and placed them on the sheet, coat each with egg glaze.** Lightly sprinkle seeds or salt over each.

❯ **Bake the snakes for 12 to 15 minutes.** Serve them warm or allow them to cool if you prefer. Depending on which snakes you created, you might want to paint mustard stripes or patterns on them.

DID YOU KNOW?

How do snakes gobble down prey twice as large as their own heads? Flexible jaws allow snakes to open wide!

A smooth green snake

credit: Peter Paplanus (CC BY 2.0)

Chapter 7

TROPICAL
SAVANNAS

Tropical savannas are grasslands located near the equator, where it's hot all year. In this biome, temperatures rarely fall below 64 degrees Fahrenheit (18 degrees Celsius). The average temperature is about 80 degrees Fahrenheit (27 degrees Celsius), although it can spike to 100 degrees Fahrenheit (38 degrees Celsius).

Tropical savannas stretch over portions of Australia, India, South America, and major areas of Africa. In fact, Africa contains most of the planet's savannas. You'll find patchy expanses of lemon grass, red oats grass, and star grass here. While temperate grasslands are nearly treeless, you'll notice that scattered shrubs rise above the grasses of the savanna.

ESSENTIAL QUESTION

What happens when ecosystems change?

Unlike the desert, African savannas feature wondrous biodiversity. Ferocious carnivores, such as cheetahs, leopards, and lions, top the food chain. They hunt hoofed herbivores, including impalas and wildebeests.

Overhead, hawks benefit from a birds-eye view of smaller prey, including meerkats, reptiles, and rodents, as they scurry through grasses. Vultures swoop from the sky to gorge on **carrion**, while hippos stay cool by splashing in the river. Endangered elephant calves stick close to mothers, whose mammoth bodies shade babies as they munch on shrubs.

Mother and baby elephants

The savanna in the tropics of Australia
credit: CSIRO (CC BY 3.0)

GRASSLAND OR DESERT?

Some people describe savannas as a combination of grassland and desert. That's because there are only two seasons, both very different. For six to eight months during summer, fierce rains bombard the savanna. Luckily, the soil is porous, so it drains quickly. These rains cause an astonishing rush of growth.

After the rainy season, the weather changes dramatically, becoming very dry.

Drought transforms the landscape. Soil becomes crusty and cracked. In the dry season, lightning often strikes the savanna and ignites fires, which are quickly spread across parched grasses by violent winds. Fire and scarce water make plant growth nearly impossible. Fires don't damage the grass roots though—these remain protected underground. When the rainy season returns, the cycle of life begins anew.

An acacia tree

SAVANNA ADAPTATIONS

Flora and fauna are well adapted to harsh conditions in savannas. Grass roots grow deep into the ground and are protected by soil during fires. The grasses sprout back quickly to provide food for animals.

Some trees even have fire-resistant trunks. Africa's baobab tree, for example, boasts an immense spongy trunk. During rainy seasons, it soaks up water and stashes it away for times of drought. With thick, crinkly folds, the baobab's trunk is well-protected against fierce flames. In addition, the baobab sprouts leaves only during the rainy season.

Speaking of leaves, the acacia tree has some delicious ones. But they're high up near the top of these umbrella-like trees. The only animals that can reach them are giraffes, nature's tallest animals. These long-necked mammals, with prehensile tongues, are well adapted to nibble sky-high greens. Lower down, sharp thorns on the trunk ward off other hungry herbivores.

WORDS TO KNOW

tendon: tissue that connects muscles to bones.

symbiosis: a relationship between two different species of organisms in which each benefits from the other.

beneficial: having good or helpful results.

pollinate: to transfer pollen from the male parts of the plant to the female parts.

parasite: a small insect or other living thing that infects a larger animal and lives off it.

gaping: an adaptation in which a crocodile opens its mouth to regulate heat.

precarious: risky or dangerous.

Halfway around the world, the savanna of the Australian Outback is full of animals that survive on very little water, such as wallabies and kangaroos. With brawny hind legs, kangaroos leap 30 feet and move at 20 to 30 miles per hour, the speed at which cars travel on many city streets.

Does it sound exhausting? Kangaroos actually use very little energy when they hop, thanks to large **tendons** in their legs. Jumbo feet aren't just for hopping, either. When a kangaroo senses danger, it sounds the alarm by thump-thump-thumping its feet on the ground.

ADAPTED FOR SAFETY

Animals grazing in wide-open spaces are easy targets for predators. What survival strategies do these animals use? Some, such as zebras, find safety in numbers. When a herd gallops together, black-and-white stripes blend together into one mass. A confused lion can't tell one zebra from another.

Others, such as giraffes, gazelles, and antelope, use long legs to quickly sprint away from roaring lions, wild dogs, and fires. It's hard to outrun the cheetah, though. The speediest land mammal in the world, the spotted cheetah dashes at 70 miles per hour. Faster than speed limits on many highways!

Watch a cheetah in action on the savanna. How is the cheetah different from a housecat? WARNING: This video contains a scene of animal death.

PS

Smithsonian cheetah video

SYMBIOSIS: A WIN-WIN SITUATION

Life in an ecosystem isn't just about predators and prey. There's plenty of cooperation, too, through **symbiosis**. Symbiosis occurs when animals or plants of differing species interact in partnerships **beneficial** for both. A win-win situation!

For example, hummingbirds get delicious nectar from flowers, but they return the favor by **pollinating**. And if you crawl on your belly to peek through the savanna brush, you might observe a red-billed oxpecker perched between an antelope's curved horns. As the antelope grazes, so does the bird—by plucking pesky **parasites**, ticks, and flies right from the herbivore's head! In a relationship that benefits both animals, the oxpecker scarfs up fast food while the antelope enjoys a speedy grooming.

DID YOU KNOW?

Vultures are sloppy eaters. They dive right into gooey carrion. Good thing the messy birds have bald heads! Otherwise, feathers would get mussed.

The Nile crocodile and the spur-winged plover, a bird with spindly legs, are another twosome. To beat savanna heat when basking in the sun, the croc unhinges its cavernous mouth. It's an adaptation called **gaping**. That's just the wide-open opportunity the plover needs to drop in for dinner. The plover alights between the fearsome predator's jaws. From its **precarious** perch, the plover digs out parasites and nibbles tasty tidbits of leftover meat trapped between the crocodile's pointy teeth. The croc, meanwhile, gets a nice teeth cleaning!

The oxpecker also provides tick removal for rhinos, wildebeests, and giraffes.
credit: Derek Keats (CC BY 2.0)

THREATS TO THE SAVANNA

One of the greatest risks to the savanna is **poaching**, or illegal hunting. The savanna contains many endangered animals. Although laws protect these animals, some people disobey the law to make money. For example, people poach elephants and rhinos for their valuable ivory tusks and horns. Sometimes, hunters set fire to the savanna to make it easier to spot prey.

Aggressive farming, overgrazing, erosion, and desertification also threaten the savanna.

Fertile lands become battered and dry and subject to drought. When people allow livestock to overgraze, grazed areas don't have time to recover and soil is unable to produce new growth. That reduces the amount of vegetation for animals to munch on. In addition, they chomp off plants that hold soil in place. Soil erosion leads to desertification.

Now, let's put a coat on and explore one of the coldest biomes—the tundra!

ESSENTIAL QUESTION

What happens when ecosystems change?

Savanna Battle

Guy Midgley is a noted South African climate researcher. He states, "Savannas are the result of a battle for living space between grasses and trees that neither side has won." Are trees now gaining an edge on grasses? The world's tropical savannas are rapidly changing as levels of carbon dioxide in the atmosphere increase. Ecosystems have grown woodier and are more **hospitable** to trees and shrubs, rather than grasses. What does that mean for the biome? Trees require more rainwater to thrive—they suck up scarce water supplies. But that's not all. Trees compete with grasses for sunlight—and claim a height advantage!

HONEY WHEAT BREAD

One of the world's most popular grains, wheat grows in the fertile soils of grasslands. It also grows in savannas, along with cotton, sugar cane, and sorghum. Gather ingredients to whip up this delicious bread with whole wheat flour. This makes two loaves, approximately 16 slices per loaf.

Caution: Have an adult help with the oven.

Ingredients

2 packages yeast	½ cup wheat germ (optional)
½ cup water	2 tablespoons wheat gluten (optional)
2 cups fat-free milk	3 cups whole wheat flour, divided
¼ cup butter	4 cups bread flour, divided
⅓ cup honey	non-stick spray
¼ cup brown sugar	melted butter
2½ teaspoons salt	

❯ **In a large mixing bowl, dissolve the yeast in the water** by stirring with a wooden spoon. Allow the yeast to stand for 10 minutes.

❯ **In the meantime, warm milk in a pot until it reaches 110 degrees Fahrenheit** (43 degrees Celsius) or a low simmer. With the wooden spoon, stir in the butter, honey, brown sugar, and salt. Pour the mixture into the large bowl containing the yeast.

❯ **Add wheat germ and wheat gluten if you're including them.** Add 2 cups of whole wheat flour and 3 cups of the bread flour. With an electric mixer, beat the mixture for 3 full minutes.

❯ **Stir in the rest of the whole wheat flour,** and add as much bread flour as you need to make a sticky dough. Place the dough on a floured board. Knead it for 10 full minutes, until the dough becomes smooth and elastic.

WORDS TO KNOW

project continues on next page . . .

sorghum: an important cereal crop grown in tropical areas, often used to feed livestock.

❱ **Spray another mixing bowl with the non-stick spray.** Place dough in the bowl, then turn it over so the top is coated with spray. Cover dough with a dish towel or pastry cloth. Allow it to rise in a warm place for about 75 minutes, until it has doubled in size.

❱ **Punch down the dough.** Let it stand for 10 minutes. Then divide the dough in two. Use the rolling pin to shape each hunk of dough into a 9-inch-by-14-inch rectangle. Begin at the short end and tightly roll the dough. Pinch the ends to seal them.

❱ **Spray two loaf pans with non-stick spray.** Then place one loaf of dough in each. Cover each with a cloth or towel. Allow them to rise in a warm place for one hour. Preheat the oven to 375 degrees Fahrenheit (190 degrees Celsius).

❱ **Bake for about 35 minutes** or until the bread sounds hollow when you gently tap it with your fingers. If you prefer the bread to remain golden brown, cover it with foil for the last 15 minutes of baking. Otherwise, the crust will darken.

❱ **Remove the loaves from the pans and brush with melted butter.** Allow them to cool before serving or storing.

Chapter 8

TUNDRA

Bundle up when you explore Earth's frostiest biome, the tundra. Here, biodiversity is low, soil is poor, and rainfall is scarce—less than 10 inches per year. The tundra experiences only two seasons—winter and summer. Winters are bitterly cold, with temperatures plummeting to -40 degrees Fahrenheit (-40 degrees Celsius), while summers warm only to about 64 degrees Fahrenheit (18 degrees Celsius).

Did you know there are three areas of tundra: **alpine**, Arctic, and Antarctic? This treeless biome is a big frosty circle at the poles of the planet and on top of tall mountain peaks. The tundra covers about 14 percent of Earth's landmass in the northern Arctic areas of Alaska, Canada, Greenland, and Siberia. These regions in the Northern Hemisphere are called Arctic tundra.

ESSENTIAL QUESTION

In the interconnected web of life, how do warming temperatures in the Arctic impact the planet?

WORDS TO KNOW

alpine: high-altitude.

timberline: also called the treeline, the altitude or limit beyond which trees do not grow in mountains or northern latitudes.

altitude: the height of land above the level of the sea.

permafrost: permanently frozen subsoil and rock just beneath the surface of the ground.

active layer: the layer of permafrost that melts in the summer.

Located on mountains above the **timberline** where no trees grow is alpine tundra. Perhaps you have hiked to a high enough **altitude** in the mountains and gone above the treeline? Chances are good that you were in alpine tundra!

It is not only in the Northern Hemisphere that you will you shiver in the tundra. Although most of Antarctica is considered a dry desert, a stretch of tundra is present along its coasts. Fittingly, it's known as Antarctic tundra.

DID YOU KNOW?

The word *tundra* comes from the Finnish word *tunturia*, which means "treeless plain."

Arctic ice

credit: Patrick Kelley (CC BY 2.0)

What characterizes tundra? **Permafrost**. It's exactly what it sounds like—a layer of permanently frozen subsoil just beneath the surface of the ground. You won't encounter permafrost in warmer biomes. In summer months, when the weather warms up, the top layer, or **active layer**, of permafrost thaws. The rest, however, remains frozen. It never defrosts. When the active layer melts, it supplies a rich ecosystem for animals, plants, and insects. Then, as winter approaches again, the active layer refreezes.

Unfortunately, as the earth's temperatures rise, the depth that thaws increases. Decomposing materials release more carbon dioxide into the atmosphere, and the greenhouse effect gets stronger.

Watch this video about the North Pole. The North Pole has no real land. It's just a colossal slab of ice! How did humans adapt to life in the Arctic?

🔍 PS

🔎 Nat Geo North Pole video

ADAPTED FOR EXTREMELY SHORT GROWING SEASONS

You've already learned that plants are the primary producers of the food chain. Without plants, animals can't survive. In the Arctic tundra, plants have to deal with an extremely short growing season—the shortest on the planet. The season is only about 50 days long, shorter than a summer break from school!

With chilly soil and not much time to carry out photosynthesis, how do plants do what they need to do?

Many, such as grasses, lichens, mosses, and shrubs, stay small. They hug the ground to avoid bitter winds. Close to the ground, carpets of short plants absorb the sun's heat, which is reflected from soil.

WORDS TO KNOW

subnivean: the ground area below a layer of snow and above soil.

insulate: to keep the heat in and the cold out.

blubber: an insulating layer of fat underneath an animal's skin that helps keep the animal warm.

The purple saxifrage flower of Denali, Alaska, has adapted to its inhospitable environment. One of the first tundra flowers to bloom when temperatures heat up, it often makes its cheery appearance as snow melts. A cushion plant, saxifrage grows in a ground-hugging cluster that looks like a pillow. It sets down deep roots in crevices between rocks, which absorb the sun's energy.

ADAPTED FOR BITTERLY COLD TEMPERATURES

Many animals avoid the frigid Arctic winters, when food is scarce, by migrating south to warmer climates. Immense herds of lichen-loving caribou move to forest biomes. Other animals, such as the singing vole, thrive in the **subnivean** layer. There, they nibble on roots and stems. Some animals, such as the Arctic ground squirrel and the grizzly bear, hibernate.

Many animals stay outside and brave the elements.

Tundra carpet
credit: Andrea Pokrzywinski (CC BY 2.0)

Have you ever bundled up in a puffy winter jacket on a freezing day? It **insulates** you against winds and frosty temperatures. For animals, **blubber** does the same thing. Blubber is a thick layer of fat located just beneath the skin that provides insulation for tundra dwellers.

Polar bear mother and young
credit: U.S. Fish and Wildlife Service Headquarters (CC BY 2.0)

For tundra animals, woolly coats are essential. Polar bears, seals, and walruses depend on woolly coats and blubber to protect them against the cold, both on land and in water.

Bigger bodies, shorter legs, and smaller ears combine to help Arctic mammals and birds survive. Compare, for instance, the Arctic rabbit with the jackrabbit of the desert biome. Instead of oversized ears that allow heat to escape like the jackrabbit's, the Arctic hare has short ears to conserve heat. A gray color in the summer, the Arctic hare turns white in the winter to camouflage itself against the snowy environment. The Arctic fox, ermine, and willow ptarmigan do the same thing.

THREATS TO THE TUNDRA

One threat to the tundra is oil drilling. Oil drilling causes air, land, water, and noise pollution. The racket disrupts wildlife and sends animals fleeing in search of peace and quiet. Oil spills are disastrous, ruining the environment and killing animals on land and in the water.

DID YOU KNOW?

The willow ptarmigan is Alaska's state bird. How does this bird tackle winter? It dive-bombs into a mound of powdery snow to keep warm and duck out of predators' view. Plunging into its shelter from above means the bird leaves no telltale tracks.

WORDS TO KNOW

radically: drastically; profoundly.

amplification: magnification.

glacier: an enormous mass of frozen snow and ice that moves across the earth's surface.

Climate change impacts the Arctic more quickly and radically than any other place on the planet.

In recent years, the Arctic has experienced record heat. Temperatures there are climbing at two to three times the global average. This is called Arctic **amplification**.

Save the Seeds!

In 2008 a team of scientists in Norway built a storage vault by chiseling into the permafrost of a frigid Arctic mountain. They intended it to protect human food supplies and crops forever. This global food bank stored representative plant seeds from the world's precious supply. It shielded the earth's plants in case of catastrophe, such as disease or the effects of continued global warming. The seed vault held samples of 208,000 plants from across the planet. It was large enough to stockpile 2 billion of the world's seeds.

Permafrost and thick rock, scientists initially thought, would safeguard the seeds. No power was needed. The vault would be impenetrable, even if the climate continued to warm. But in 2016, just eight years later, global warming whooshed in extreme weather. Soaring temperatures in the Arctic launched heavy rains. And the failsafe permafrost unexpectedly melted! Meltwater breached the entry of the tunnel that leads to the doomsday vault. It froze into ice, which scientists had to hack away. Fortunately, water didn't get into the vault, and the seeds remained protected.

In 2018, Norway announced plans to spend 100 million Norwegian crowns (13 million dollars) to upgrade the seed vault. Workers will build a concrete tunnel and dig trenches into the mountainsides. Trenches will act as channels to keep meltwater away from the vault.

DID YOU KNOW?

How many gallons of oil do people across the globe consume each day? About 96 million barrels. That's about 35 billion barrels a year!

What causes Arctic amplification? Think about the ways you beat the heat in sizzling temperatures. Do you wear white clothes? In light colors, you keep cool and comfy because they reflect more sunlight. Dark colors absorb sunlight and turn it into heat. It works the same way in the ocean.

When temperatures rise, sea ice thins and melts. Sea ice is light-colored. It's bright and reflects sunlight. When it melts, dark ocean waters are revealed. Dark waters absorb more sunlight and heat, instead of bouncing energy back into space.

Earth's higher temperatures cause Arctic ice to melt and **glaciers** to shrink. Polar bears can't find enough food to survive. Thin and unhealthy, mother polar bears can't produce enough milk to feed their young. Many bears attempt to swim great distances in search of food and new habitats, but not all of them make it.

Brrr! Now that your nose is frozen, let's go someplace a little warmer—but not much! It's time to climb some mountains.

ESSENTIAL QUESTION

In the interconnected web of life, how do warming temperatures in the Arctic impact the planet?

CONDUCT A SEED SPEED RACE

How does freezing affect a seed's ability to germinate? Find out when you conduct a Seed Speed Race.

❯ **Use fast-growing seeds, such as beans.** Tally the total number of seeds you have and divide that number in half. Place half of the seeds in a resealable freezer bag and place the bag into a freezer. Set aside the other seeds and keep them at room temperature. Wait 24 hours.

❯ **Write "First Frozen" on one plastic tub or container.** Write "Not Frozen" on another. Fill the containers about halfway with potting soil. Place the frozen seeds in the soil of the first tub and the not frozen seeds in the soil of the second tub. Add more soil until each tub or container is about three-quarters full.

❯ **Place the tubs of seeds next to each other in a sunny location.** Start a scientific method worksheet in your journal and predict what will happen to the seeds. Do you think one set will germinate faster than the other? Why or why not?

❯ **Water—but don't drown—the seeds every day for 10 days.** Notice their progress above and below the soil. Jot down your observations in your journal. Sketch the stages of growth you observe.

❯ **Which set of seeds, if either, won the Seed Speed Race?** What conclusions can you draw about the effects of freezing on seeds?

DID YOU KNOW?

In 2015, civil war destroyed a seed bank in Aleppo, Syria. Researchers in Syria withdrew seeds from Norway's vault and regrew their own supplies.

Try This!

Repeat the experiment with different seeds. Predict whether your results will be different or the same, and test your predictions.

WORDS TO KNOW

germinate: to begin to grow from a seed.

TEST YOUR AIR QUALITY

Arctic haze is a certain kind of polar air mass. Chock-full of chemical pollutants from Canada, Eurasia, and the United States, this reddish-brown smog sometimes hangs over Alaska, creating poor air quality. What's the air quality like where you live? Conduct this test to find out.

❯ **Choose four separate areas, both indoors and outdoors**, to test the air. Indoors, you might select your kitchen, and outdoors, target a bush or shrub. Start a scientific method worksheet and write each location on a separate page in your science journal, for example, "On Kitchen Windowsill" or "Next to Azalea Bush."

❯ **Label one index card for each location.** Your labels should match those in your science journal. Use a craft stick to spread petroleum jelly over the cards. Leave each card in a safe spot in its target area. Wait 8 hours.

❯ **To collect data, visit each location and gather its card.** Use a magnifying glass to study each sample. Do you observe any particles? What color are they? Can you identify what they are? Record your findings in your science journal.

❯ **While you're at each location, use your senses to take in your surroundings.** In your journal, write your observations of the area on the correct page. Can you smell anything? Does the air feel dusty or damp? Do you see blowing sand or plant parts? Is there cigarette smoke, industrial **emissions**, or road construction that are affecting air quality?

❯ **Place each sample in a row.** Use the magnifying glass to compare and contrast each card. Which sample is the cleanest? The dirtiest? What conclusions can you draw about the air quality?

Think About It

Saharan sunsets occur when gigantic dust clouds from Africa's Sahara Desert travel thousands of miles across the globe. These produce hazy skies, hotter temperatures, allergies—and beautiful sunsets.

WORDS TO KNOW

emission: something sent or given off, such as smoke, gas, heat, or light.

MAKE YOUR OWN GLACIER

A glacier is a gargantuan mass of compacted snow and solid ice. Formed in the Arctic and Antarctic thousands of years ago, glaciers also develop outside these areas on mountain peaks and valleys. As snow thaws and freezes again, glaciers thicken and continue to grow.

Slowly but continuously, glaciers move. In fact, people have called glaciers "rivers of ice" since they constantly move like water. As glaciers advance or increase in size and move forward, they haul boulders and push mounds of rock debris in front of them. As they retreat, or melt, glaciers deposit boulders in new places. They create lakes, carve craggy hills, and etch valleys into the landscape. Make your own glacier and see how it moves!

❯ **Use a milk carton or other container.** With scissors, carefully cut away one of its side panels.

❯ **Fill about one-third of the carton with gravel, rocks, and sand to form rock debris.** Pour in enough water to cover the rock debris, and stir. Place the carton into a freezer and allow it to freeze solid.

❯ **When the carton is completely frozen, remove it from the freezer.** Fill another third of the carton with the same gravel, rocks, sand, and water mixture. Return the carton to the freezer, and allow it to freeze solid again. Your glacier will grow larger and thicker.

❯ **When the carton has thoroughly frozen again, remove it from the freezer.** In the remaining one-third of the carton, add the same gravel, rocks, sand, and water mixture. Place the carton in the freezer again, and let your glacier bulk up even more.

❯ **Select a day when the outside temperature is above 55 degrees Fahrenheit** (13 degrees Celsius) and below 80 degrees Fahrenheit (27 degrees Celsius). Now, you're ready to take your glacier outside and observe its movement.

❯ **Outdoors, position a wooden board or panel at a 20-degree angle.** At the top of the board, spread a 1-inch layer of gravel. Peel and pull away the cardboard portions of the carton. Place your frozen glacier at the top of the board. Wait about an hour.

❯ **Observe how the glacier has moved across the board.** What happened to the gravel? How much ice has melted? Has any rock debris been left behind? What formations do you notice?

DID YOU KNOW?

Penguins plop onto their bellies to slide over icy snow! Can you tell why this sliding is called tobogganing? Wheeee!

Try This!

New life blooms from an Ice Age flower! More than 32,000 years ago in Siberia, Ice Age Arctic ground squirrels filled their hibernation burrows. The rodents stashed fruit from a narrow-leaf campion, a white flower. Over millennia, permafrost preserved the ancient plant tissues, which never thawed. The fruit remained buried in permafrost until 2012, when a team of Russian scientists from the Institute of Cells Biophysics near Moscow excavated the burrow. Read about the scientists who regenerated the frozen tissues, and share the incredible story with a friend or family member.

🔎 regenerated flowers discover mag

Chapter 9

MOUNTAINS

Ready to trek through steep and rocky mountain ranges? Mountains tower over every continent, covering 20 percent of the earth's land surface. They also rise from the floors of each of the planet's oceans.

Some scientists don't consider mountains a separate biome. Mountain ranges often contain other biomes. Mountain ranges create **ecotones**, where one biome transitions into another. For example, the lower slopes of mountains often include waving grasslands or vast deserts. Deciduous forests often cover **foothills**. As you **ascend**, you'll move through coniferous forests that bathe a mountain in lush green. Higher up, tundra landscapes above the treeline paint peaks snowy white in winter—and sometimes all year long.

ESSENTIAL QUESTION

What makes mountains different from other biomes?

Despite the multi-ecoregion nature of mountains, some scientists classify them as distinct biomes. They point out that certain wildlife, such as the Himalayan marmot, live only in particular mountain areas. As with other biomes, mountain ranges contain a variety of water ecosystems: ponds, streams, wetlands, rivers, and lakes.

MOUNTAIN FORMATION

Mountain ranges formed through **geological events** during millions of years. The earth's surface is made of **tectonic plates** that constantly drift. When plates crash into one another, pressure causes some land to sink. Other land lifts, crinkles, or forms a **fault**. When melted rock surges through cracked areas, volcanic activities can occur. As time passes, ice, water, and wind erosion carve out breathtaking landscapes.

Rocky Mountain National Park
credit: National Park Service Digital Image Archives

WORDS TO KNOW

life zones: ecological communities.

montane: the mountain zone located below 8,000 feet.

subalpine: the mountain zone located at 8,000 to 11,500 feet.

krummholz line: the highest altitude where stunted trees grow.

flagging: trees with needles and branches on only one side.

perennial: a plant that flowers and lives for more than one season.

annual: a plant that flowers and dies in one season. New ones grow the next year from seeds.

LIFE ZONES

Climate varies in mountains. As you climb higher and higher up a single mountain, you experience dropping temperatures. Soil becomes different as you trudge up. You also spot changing vegetation and different animals.

Depending where you are in the world, you'll encounter different **life zones** on mountains. Life zones have specific ecological communities and locations on mountains. Altitude, soil, levels of dryness or wetness, and types of vegetation all influence life zones.

In North America's Rocky Mountains, for example, the three main life zones are **montane**, **subalpine**, and alpine. The montane level is located below 8,000 feet. It's the warmest and driest zone and is the most hospitable to people and wildlife. Aspen trees, blue spruce, Douglas firs, and lodgepole pines are common here.

You'll find the subalpine zone at an elevation of 8,000 to 11,500 feet. Trees, mostly firs and spruces, are shorter and more scattered. Towering above 11,500 feet is the alpine zone, where wildflowers and squat shrubs hug the ground. High winds and a short growing season make conditions difficult for plants. Just how difficult are growing conditions? As you near what's called the **krummholz line** high on a mountain, you might see twisty, gnarled trees that resemble shrubs.

Powerful winds cause these dwarfed trees to bend sideways and prevent them from growing upright.

DID YOU KNOW?

Himalayan marmots, members of the squirrel family and kin to prairie dogs, live at mind-boggling altitudes of 10,000 to 14,000 feet! These grass-gnawing rodents are nicknamed "whistle pigs." They whistle shrilly to alert their pals when predators snoop around.

Although you might spot scattered tall spruce trees, you'll notice they have branches and needles on only one side—like a flag. This phenomenon, called **flagging**, is a result of winds that constantly pummel trees.

To survive in such harsh conditions, alpine plants are **perennials**, plants that live through several growing seasons. Perennials don't expend precious energy to grow stems and leaves in one season, the way **annuals** do.

ADAPTED TO THE HIGH LIFE

Are you feeling a little bit loopy up here? It's the air! Mountain air is thin and cold and contains little oxygen. The higher the altitude, the more challenging it becomes for animals to survive. Let's take a look at how some marvelous mountain mammals strut their stuff.

The pine marten of the Rocky Mountains is a member of the weasel family. This little predator sports a cat-like face and ears. It sprouts extra fur on toe pads to keep its feet toasty as it scurries over snow. Remember the desert's fennec fox, which grows thick fur to shield its feet on scorching sands? This is a similar adaptation for surviving a different environment.

A brown yak

How does the threatened yak adapt to thin air in the high altitudes of Asia's Himalayas? This shaggy member of the ox family boasts a burly chest with huge lungs that allow it to inhale hefty amounts of air. A fleecy outer coat and a downy inner one provide a double layer of protection against the unforgiving region, where temperatures plunge to -40 degrees Fahrenheit (-40 degrees Celsius).

Mountainous terrain is also often tricky. In the Andes of Peru, sure-footed llamas navigate treacherous terrain. Double-toed feet with leathery bottom pads prevent them from stumbling.

The 2-ounce pygmy tarsier would fit in the palm of your hand! With oversized eyes and ears, this teeny nocturnal primate swivels its head 180 degrees like an owl. Scientists believed the pygmy tarsier became extinct in 1921, after people cleared away much of its habitat. In 2008, scientists were thrilled to encounter four live tarsiers in the mountains of Indonesia. But these carnivorous primates are hard to find, and their mountainous habitat is dwindling. Today, scientists aren't sure of the number of pygmy tarsiers in the wild and consider their status unknown.

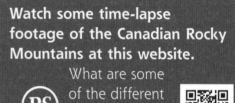

Watch some time-lapse footage of the Canadian Rocky Mountains at this website. What are some of the different life zones that you spot?

PS

mountains in motion

Tarsier with branch
credit: Kok Leng Yeo (CC BY 2.0)

CLIMATE CHANGE THREATS

In China, pandas are a symbol of peace. Sadly, the giant panda totters on the brink of extinction. Increasing human populations need more land. People have cleared away the panda's habitat to obtain logs for fuel and land for rice farms. In doing so, they also cleared away the bamboo plants that pandas feast on.

Giant panda munching bamboo
credit: Chen Wu (CC BY 2.0)

Most of the world's remaining wild panda populations live in China's Qinling and Minshan Mountains, where bamboo grows on the forest floor. Giant pandas gobble bamboo stems, shoots, and leaves. In fact, bamboo is nearly the only food pandas eat. It makes up 99 percent of their diet. With bamboo providing little nutritional value, pandas must forage for about 26 to 84 pounds a day. That's a lot of green stuff! In a fragile habitat, that food source is shriveling.

DID YOU KNOW?

The giant panda has an oily coating on its woolly fur. This adaptation is like a waterproof raincoat that keeps pandas warm in China's mountains.

In 2018, a scientific study published in the journal *Nature Climate Change* predicted climate change will destroy the bamboo needed by the giant pandas. The study concluded that panda habitats might be wiped out by the end of this century.

Fortunately, the Chinese government is committed to action. Working with scientists, researchers, universities, and organizations including the World Wildlife Fund (WWF), China has increased and restored panda habitats.

From land to sea, it's time to head to a very watery biome—the ocean!

ESSENTIAL QUESTION

What makes mountains different from other biomes?

MAKE YOUR OWN ERUPTING VOLCANO

When magma, or molten rock, busts through the earth's crust, it splits and cracks rocks. Fiery volcanoes erupt, spewing fountains of lava, toxic gases, and choking ash. Create your own volcano and experience its eruption!

➤ **Use your favorite recipe for making modeling dough.** Allow the dough to cool until it is safe to knead thoroughly. Roll the dough into a ball, and wrap it in foil to keep it from drying out.

➤ **Cut a cardboard tube to about 8 inches in length.** Use some modeling dough to plug one end of the tube. Use masking tape to fasten the tube, plugged side on the bottom, to a sturdy piece of cardboard.

➤ **Crinkle newspaper into balls of different sizes.** Tape the newspaper balls all around the tube and over the cardboard. Place larger wads of paper at the bottom of the volcano and smaller ones at the top to form a cone shape.

➤ **Use the modeling dough to cover the volcano.** Make sure to leave the top of the tube uncovered. Paint your volcano to look like a rocky volcano cone. Allow everything to dry overnight.

➤ **When the volcano is dry, pour baking soda into the cardboard tube** so that it's at least halfway full. Add a few drops of red food coloring to 8 ounces of vinegar so your molten lava will look authentic.

➤ **Now, take your volcano outside for the eruption.** Wear goggles as you pour the vinegar into the cardboard tube. Step away from the volcano and watch it erupt!

Think About It

Scientists have discovered fossils of seashells on Mount Everest, the world's tallest mountain. How can that be? At one time, millions of years ago, the ocean covered the land where Everest now towers.

EXPERIMENT WITH WATER EROSION

Erosion occurs naturally through the action of glaciers, water, and wind. It contributes to spectacular mountain scenery. Let's simulate erosion and watch nature's sculptor in action!

❯ **Go outside and use sand to create three little hills on a sidewalk, driveway, or paved area.** Leave about 12 inches between each hill. Press the sand hills tightly on their sides, as if you're packing a snowball or mudball. Place four toothpicks in the sides of each hill. Sprinkle grass clippings or shredded paper over the first sand hill. The toothpicks should still peek out. Leave the other two hills.

❯ **Start a scientific method worksheet and sketch and label each of the hills in your journal.** Predict what will happen to the first two hills during a light rainfall. How will the grass or paper influence the outcome? What will happen to the toothpicks? Jot down your predictions.

❯ **Use a watering can to cause light rainfall by sprinkling a small amount of water on the first and second sand hills.** What happens to the toothpicks? How much sand flushes away? Do the grass clippings or shredded paper prevent erosion, slow it down, or speed it up?

❯ **You have a lone sand hill left.** Predict what will happen to it in a heavy rainfall, and write down your prediction.

❯ **Now, use the sprinkling can or hose to create the rainfall.** Pour a large amount of water on the sand hill. What happens to the toothpicks? How much sand flushes away? How does it compare to what happened to the previous two hills? What conclusions can you draw about your experiment?

Think About It

How did your results compare with those you experienced in your experiment with Erosion Vessels on page 37?

Chapter 10

OCEANS

Let's take a quick dip in the ocean, or marine biome, the largest of all biomes. Earth is a watery world. It's nicknamed the "Blue Planet" because water covers about 71 percent of its surface.

Do you live near an ocean? The marine biome is the saltwater surrounding all the continents. It includes the Arctic, Atlantic, Indian, Pacific, and Southern Oceans. Ocean waters never stop moving. Constant ocean motion is driven by wind and by Earth's **rotation** as it spins.

When wind blows over the ocean, it transfers energy to the water's surface and thrusts water away. Water changes shape, forming frothy waves. Depending on wind speed, wave size varies. A light breeze ruffles the ocean with gentle fingers, while a storm's powerful gusts create towering whitewater peaks.

ESSENTIAL QUESTION

How does ocean depth impact biodiversity?

Currents are masses of water always on the move. Surface ocean currents are caused by winds and Earth's rotation. Currents move in a particular path, flowing in swirling motions.

In the Northern Hemisphere, circular currents flow in a clockwise direction. In the Southern Hemisphere, currents move **counterclockwise**. Some scientists compare ocean currents to streams or rivers within the ocean.

Have you ever swallowed a bit of ocean water? How did it taste? During millions of years, freshwater from rainfall, rivers, and streams washed over the earth's rocks. Some rocks have a lot of salt in them, and salt dissolves in water. Water washed salt away from the rocks and into the sea. No wonder the ocean tastes salty!

WORDS TO KNOW

marine: found in the ocean or having to do with the ocean.

rotation: turning around a fixed point.

current: the steady flow of water or air in one direction.

counterclockwise: the direction that goes opposite to the hands of a clock.

DID YOU KNOW?

The world's largest creature, the endangered blue whale, inhabits waters of the sunlight zone. This beautiful behemoth weighs a massive 150 tons and stretches to an astonishing 100 feet in length. If a blue whale could stand on its tail, it would be as tall as the Lincoln Memorial in Washington, DC!

zone: an area of the ocean based on depth.

sunlight zone: the ocean zone that sunlight penetrates, where photosynthesis can occur and plants can grow.

TEMPERATURES AND ZONES

Although water in the marine biome is constantly moving and mixing, water temperatures vary, depending on location. Polar waters, in the far north and south near the poles, are as low as a frosty 28 degrees Fahrenheit (-2 degrees Celsius). Tropical waters close to the equator are typically 85 degrees Fahrenheit (29 degrees Celsius).

Ocean depth also impacts temperatures. The temperature on the ocean floor is drastically colder than at the surface.

Biodiversity and adaptations also change with ocean depth. Imagine you're traveling into the ocean, farther and farther from shore, into deeper and darker waters. Eventually, the floor drops dramatically.

DID YOU KNOW?

An aquanaut is an underwater explorer. The Latin prefix *aqua* means "water." The Greek suffix comes from the word "nautical." *Naut* means "explorer or voyager." What other words do you know that contain aqua? How about naut?

Clownfish

WHAT?! YOU'RE SAYING THAT THERE'S A RAINFOREST IN THE OCEAN? UNDERWATER?

NO, I SAID THAT SOMETIMES CORAL REEFS ARE CALLED THE "RAINFORESTS OF THE SEA!"

IT'S BECAUSE, SIMILAR TO RAINFORESTS, CORAL REEFS ARE TEEMING WITH LIFE AND BIODIVERSITY.

WELL, THAT MAKES A LOT MORE SENSE, BECAUSE I'M PRETTY SURE THAT THAT IT NEVER RAINS UNDERWATER.

Scientists divide the ocean into **zones**, or levels, according to depth and the amount of sunlight each zone receives. When you splash in waters at an ocean shore, you're in the **sunlight zone**. Not surprisingly, this clear, bright zone features the greatest biodiversity.

You've learned that plants require sunlight to perform photosynthesis. In the sunlight zone, seagrasses and algae thrive. Close to 90 percent of the ocean's living things inhabit the sunlight zone. That's why brightly colored coral reefs, teeming with life, are called "rainforests of the sea." Here, you'll find seals, sea turtles, sharks, lobsters, crabs, and brilliantly colored fish.

Water, Water, Everywhere!

Water vapor, liquid water, ice. Water vapor is above us in clouds and air. On Earth's surface, oceans hold a whopping 96.5 percent of our water. Rivers, lakes, swamps, and even moist soil in the ground hold fresh water. So do icecaps and glaciers. How much water is there in all? And where is it located?

Explore drawings, charts, and graphs from USGS, the United States Geological Survey, to learn about the planet's saline water and freshwater resources. Share your findings with a friend or family member.

 USGS how much water

WORDS TO KNOW

limestone: a kind of rock that forms from the skeletons and shells of sea creatures.

polyps: small creatures that live in colonies and form coral.

calcium carbonate: a mineral found in animal bones that forms limestone.

twilight zone: the ocean zone reached by some sunlight, but not enough to allow photosynthesis to occur.

wary: feeling or showing caution about possible dangers.

RAINFORESTS OF THE SEA

You've learned that symbiosis is a win-win partnership between plants and animals of differing species. Colorful coral reefs are amazing examples of symbiosis. They are a combination of living animals and the skeletons of dead ones.

Have you ever discovered a chunk of coral washed up on a beach? It looks like a lump of rock with lots of holes. Coral is actually a kind of **limestone**. That's rock formed from shells and skeletons of marine animals. These incredible water rainforests start with microscopic, tentacled animals called coral **polyps**. The polyp attaches itself to an underwater rock. Algae live within cells of coral. Algae use coral for protection and supply it with food.

Take a tour of the Great Barrier Reef in this video!

Why is important to take care of places such as this?

🔍 Nat Geo barrier reef video

Coral provides shelter for fish.

As the polyps reproduce, they create a colony. That's a group of polyps attached together. To create their own skeletons, polyps use calcium from seawater. They produce **calcium carbonate**, or limestone, over their lower bodies. In time, living polyps die— and their skeletons become part of the reef.

A striped anglerfish
credit: NOAA

Polyp skeletons are like building blocks that add onto the reef as living polyps clamp on and grow. It's a slow process, though—it takes nearly 10,000 years for a coral reef to form!

DEEPER, DARKER ZONES

As you descend into deeper waters of the **twilight zone**, you'll notice light is limited. It's lucky that deep-sea creatures are adapted with stellar eyesight! Consider the hatchet fish, with a scrunched body that resembles a small axe. Bulging, tube-shaped eyes point up so it can spot food drifting overhead. The bizarre-looking barreleye fish boasts a see-through head. Tubular eyes roll upward. The **wary** fish sees predators through its transparent head and zips to safety. Its eyes rotate forward when the barrelhead chomps on prey.

DID YOU KNOW?

Pearls are the only gems found in living creatures, protected in mollusks such as oysters. Like coral reefs, pearls are formed from calcium carbonate.

WORDS TO KNOW

midnight zone: the ocean zone where there is no sunlight.

bioluminescence: a chemical reaction that allows deep-sea creatures to produce their own light.

photophores: special organs in the bodies of deep-sea creatures that allow them to produce light.

By the time you plunge into the **midnight zone**, it's pitch-black. How do sea creatures live in total darkness? With extreme adaptations! Some deep-sea creatures survive by providing their own light in murky waters. **Bioluminescence** is an adaptation that allows both twilight and midnight zoners, such as squid, flashlight fish, and anglerfish, to glow in the dark, using special chemicals present in their bodies.

Consider the vampire squid, so named because it has webbing that flutters out from behind it like Dracula's cape. **Photophores**, organs that produce light, cover the vampire squid's body. It can turn on lights to attract both mates and prey, as well as startle and temporarily blind predators.

The ocean floor is amazing, covered with soaring mountains and vast canyons! The ocean has many submerged volcanoes that are very active, and violently so.

Take the Pacific Ocean's Ring of Fire. This boomerang-shaped stretch of volcanic activity reaches from waters off New Zealand and around the Philippines. It swings up to Alaska and down to the coasts of North and South America. The Ring of Fire hosts about 75 percent of the earth's volcanoes, both dormant and active. Underwater eruptions and earthquakes rock the waves.

Try This!

Make waves! Grab a small bowl and fill it halfway with water. Hold the bowl over a sink. Now, slowly blow over the water surface to create a light breeze. Those resulting little ripples are called cats' paws. An old sailors' superstition claimed cats became frisky when gales brewed at sea, predicting that calm breezes would turn wild. Now, blast the water with a fast puff of breath. What happens to the waves?

THREATS TO THE MARINE BIOME

Climate change threatens the earth's oceans as much as it threatens the terrestrial biomes. One example is the danger faced by coral reefs. Warmer waters stress sensitive coral. When stressed, coral tosses out algae, which provide coral's dazzling colors as well as food for survival.

The coral starves to death. Drained of vibrant color, it looks bleached. With the impact of climate change, reefs don't have proper time to recover before the next bleaching incident strikes.

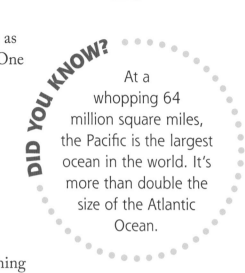

DID YOU KNOW?

At a whopping 64 million square miles, the Pacific is the largest ocean in the world. It's more than double the size of the Atlantic Ocean.

Plastic debris
credit: Kevin Krejci (CC BY 2.0)

WORDS TO KNOW

biodegrade: to decay or break down naturally.

toxin: a poisonous or harmful substance.

Carbon dioxide dissolved in ocean water weakens skeletons of corals so that they are more easily damaged. It also interferes with the formation of shells in shellfish.

Another huge threat to marine biomes drifts aimlessly in Earth's oceans, rivers, and lakes: Garbage!

We know there's water, water, everywhere. It seems we have plastic, plastic, everywhere, too. Junk we dump behind us is globally distributed in our waters—tattered plastic bags, bobbing pellets, smashed toys, and bits of plastic bottles.

DID YOU KNOW?

Plastic is forever. It never **biodegrades**. Scientists studied an albatross that died after consuming garbage. In its stomach, they discovered a bit of plastic that contained a serial number. That number came from a World War II plane that was gunned down over the Pacific Ocean in 1944.

Wind, waves, and sun break down plastic into teeny pieces. This concoction ends up in our waterways and threatens animal life. **Toxins** in plastics poison animal life. Ducks and seabirds mistakenly gobble down plastic pellets. Dolphins are entangled in bags. Trash causes severe injuries and even death through choking or clogged intestines.

In the vast, interconnected web of life, trash and pollutants in waters affect humans, too. Fish eat plant life that floats in toxic waters. Then, we eat fish that have ingested toxins. In addition, trash contaminates our beaches.

Diver Rich Horner plunged underwater off Bali's Manta Point and found . . . plastic. **View Horner's astonishing underwater footage to** (PS) **see an ocean that needs our help.**

ecowatch Rich Horner

In 2014, scientists from the group 5 Gyres published their findings on marine debris. Researchers used nets to collect plastic trash from oceans. Then, using computer models, they estimated that the world's oceans hold 5.25 trillion particles of plastic. That's about 269,000 tons of junk!

What can you do to help? First, cut down on your use of plastic products. Always recycle any plastic you can. And pitch in to pick up garbage. Your actions benefit our planet.

ESSENTIAL QUESTION

How does ocean depth impact biodiversity?

Ocean Predators

Two predators at the top of the food chain, the barracuda and shark, are adapted for hunting. Sleek and missile-shaped, the toothy twosome flit around nooks and crannies of coral reefs. Barracudas use their eyes to spot prey, such as meaty tuna and grouper. They attack with a speedy strike and use their two sets of jutting, triangular teeth to snatch and devour fish. Known for huge jaws, sharks prey on barracudas. Rather than using their eyes to spot dinner, sharks sense a prey's vibrations in water and sneak up behind or beneath their victims. Sharks boast a remarkable mouthful of choppers, too. If a shark's tooth snaps off as it gnaws prey, it's no problem. A new tooth grows to replace the lost one. Camouflage coloring is another shark adaptation. The carnivore's skin is darker on top of its body than on the bottom. Unsuspecting prey dart above a shark without seeing it. When prey swim under the predator, the shark's lighter-colored bottom camouflages it against the bright waters of the sunlight zone. Gulp!

credit: NOAA

MAKE A BLUBBER MITT

For animals such as walruses, polar bears, harp seals, and sea lions, blubber is important for survival. Blubber not only keeps animals warm, but also provides them with buoyancy. Make a blubber mitt to discover how this remarkable fat works to insulate and protect animals.

❱ **Slip on a plastic glove.** Then, spread about 1 tablespoon of lard or vegetable shortening on top of the glove—across the back of the hand and inside the palm.

❱ **Pull a second glove over the lard-covered glove.** To prevent lard from oozing out and water from seeping in later, fold the cuff of the bottom glove over the top glove. If you don't have plastic gloves, you can use plastic bags. With your free hand, position the lard so it's evenly spread over your gloved hand.

❱ **What do you predict will happen when you plunge both hands into a tub of ice water?** Test it out! Lard acts as an insulator. It protects your hand from experiencing the coldness of the water, while keeping your body heat from escaping.

❱ **Have a friend or family member use a stopwatch or simply count to determine how many seconds you keep each hand in water.** How do the times compare? Did you feel any cold through the blubber mitt? What conclusions can you draw about blubber?

Think About It

Humpback whales, which rely on dwindling Antarctic krill supplies, are becoming thinner and losing blubber. With continued warming temperatures, how might the future whale population be impacted? What will happen to the weaker whales and their abilities to migrate long distances to feed?

WORDS TO KNOW

buoyancy: the ability to float.

Chapter 11

WHAT GOES AROUND
COMES AROUND

Whew! You've finished your journey around the world and are right back where you started, in your own backyard. Use your knowledge of biomes to consider your role in the web of life. Some biomes seem remote, as if you couldn't possibly have an impact on them. But in the interconnected global environment, what goes around comes around. You can be like a domino that starts a ripple effect of positive influences on the planet!

In the last 100 years, the earth's temperature has risen by 1.4 degrees Fahrenheit (0.8 degrees Celsius). Sounds pretty puny, doesn't it? As we've seen, though, the impact of global warming is enormous. Climate change affects the entire planet by melting ice caps and raising sea levels, parching savannas, and increasing the spread of deserts.

ESSENTIAL QUESTION

What have you discovered about Earth's vast interconnections?

WHAT CAN YOU DO?

Think about what you can do to benefit the environment. What actions can you take? How can you inspire others to do the same? Start off by reducing your carbon footprint. That's the impact your activities have on the environment when they produce carbon dioxide. Walk, pedal your bike, or roll on your skateboard whenever possible. A bonus? It's good for your body, too. When traveling longer distances, take the bus or help your family organize a carpool.

In 2017, researchers studied global plastic production data. They learned that since the 1950s, the world has made 9 billion tons of plastic. And global plastic production continues to rise.

How many cast-off plastic bottles have you spotted in your neighborhood lately? They're everywhere!

Too many people drink bottled water away from home, at places such as sporting events, amusement parks, and concerts. When crowds clear out, they leave mounds of discarded containers behind.

Try to avoid buying bottled water whenever you can. Instead, carry water in a reusable, eco-friendly container. While you're at it, don't stop with water bottles. Ask your family to swap juice boxes for larger cans or bottles, and divvy the jumbo containers into smaller, reusable ones.

Grab the bulk size instead of buying 12 single-serving bags of chips. That way, you'll cut down on packaging materials you throw away.

Does It Have to Be New?

When you slip into your favorite old hoodie, you know new doesn't necessarily mean better! Before you buy a new item, find out if you can borrow or swap something. You might also find a gently used item at a yard sale or thrift shop. Better yet, bring your creativity into play and discover a way to reuse something you already own in a whole new way, so you don't need a new one at all!

And don't forget to reuse or recycle paper, plastics, cans, and other materials you do use.

THE TOP 10

Here are 10 actions you can take right away to make a difference on Earth.

- Take showers instead of baths to conserve water. Tubs require 70 gallons of water to fill, while showers use 25 gallons on average.

- The amount of water you use in your shower depends on how long you spend there. While you're at it, shorten showers by one minute, or more than that if you take long showers. (Hey, you'll gain extra time to sleep!)

• Dentists recommend you brush your pearly whites for two full minutes, two times a day. As you brush your choppers, switch off the faucet. Why? If you run water for two minutes, you waste two gallons of water.

• Drip, drip, drip! Leaky faucet? Tightly turn it off. Don't let a valuable resource dribble down the drain.

Energy Vampires

Dastardly villains suck energy in your home 24/7. How? They endlessly guzzle electricity. Did you know that even when you switch off computers and other electronics, they still consume energy if they're plugged in? A cell phone charger uses electricity even when your phone isn't charging. Here's a quick fix. Ask an adult to plug all electronics into a single power strip. Then, flick off the strip when you've finished watching TV or using the computer.

• Collect rainwater and use it to water houseplants, your desertarium, or your hummingbird garden.

• Don't dawdle as you select a snack from the fridge. Grab the snack and close the door as quickly as you can to save energy.

• Switch off lights when you leave a room.

• Turn off all electronics when you're finished using them.

• When you enter and leave your house, shut the door quickly. The furnace or air conditioner will require less energy to do its job.

• Paper or plastic? Neither! Tote a reusable bag when you go shopping.

WHAT ELSE CAN YOU DO?

Here are five more things your family can do to help the environment and stop global warming. You can help save the planet and the biomes on it.

• Plant a tree. Trees take carbon dioxide out of the atmosphere and put oxygen into it. A tree is like your own air-purifying machine.

• Buy local products. Not only will you support your local farmer or store, but you'll also help conserve fuel required to ship products from across the country.

• Buy products with minimal packaging when possible and generate less trash. When you buy organic, you choose products grown without chemical fertilizers.

• Next time your family needs a new appliance, choose one that's energy efficient.

• Do a carbon footprint audit for your family. Check out carbonfootprint. com or other online sites. When you see how your individual actions contribute to your carbon footprint, you can take steps to change your behavior—and reduce your footprint.

By taking steps to take care of planet Earth, you are doing your part to protect its amazing biomes and all the creatures that live here!

ESSENTIAL QUESTION

What have you discovered about Earth's vast interconnections?

EXPLORE YOUR HOME TURF

You've traveled the globe and explored its biomes. Now, it's time to dig out that recycled paper you created way back at the beginning of the book. Wander into the great outdoors and take in the sights with a fresh set of eyes.

❯ **Decide on a target ecosystem to explore.** It might be a fallen log, a cactus, or a sunny patch in a grassy field.

❯ **Study the area.** What living things do you notice? Nonliving things? Do plants and animals that you see seem to demonstrate any special adaptations to their environment? Do any have camouflage? How are today's weather conditions typical of the climate in which you live? What might threaten the environment? Record observations and thoughts in your science journal.

❯ **Use a thermometer to determine the temperature.** Record it and describe the weather conditions in your journal.

❯ **Slip on gardening gloves and turn over a patch of earth.** You've investigated soil before. How does this sample compare? Jot your impressions in your science journal.

Try This!

Use a sheet of scratch paper to compose a haiku about your target ecosystem. Haiku is a traditional form of Japanese poetry that often describes and celebrates nature or the seasons. Haiku poems are not rhymed. They contain three lines with 17 syllables: five in the first line, seven in the second line, and five in the third line.

> Leaves flutter like wings
> Orange as autumn's pumpkins
> They fall in crisp piles

When you're happy with your haiku, copy it on your recycled paper and illustrate it. Share it with a friend or family member and then hang it in a special place!

DO SOME FURTHER RESEARCH

❯ **Investigate endangered animals in your state** at the U.S. Fish and Wildlife Service.

🔎 fws endangered

❯ **Wildfires are an indicator of climate change.** Read the EPA's August 2016 document, which "tracks the frequency, extent, and severity of wildfires in the United States."

🔎 wildfires EPA PDF

❯ **In winter 2018, snow fell over deserts across the world.** Visit NASA's Earth Observatory to learn more.

🔎 earth observatory NASA

❯ **One of the world's most breathtaking cities, Cape Town, is a port city on South Africa's coast.** Home to a population of nearly 440,000 people, Cape Town is an extremely popular tourist destination. And it's parched, suffering a dire water crisis brought on by prolonged, extreme drought and climate change. Research Cape Town's water crisis. How was it possible for water, a renewable resource, to run dry? What other cities across the globe may run out of drinking water, too? What will it mean for the future?

🔎 National Geographic Cape Town water

❯ **Have tropical storms become so severe** they require a new category?

🔎 real climate cyclones

❯ **Arctic ice is melting at an increasingly alarming rate.** What does it mean for our future—and our present?

🔎 PBS Antarctic ice loss

DID YOU KNOW?

By 2050, the world population will hit nearly 10 billion! How will Earth's biomes sustain food supplies for a booming population? How can we makes changes now to feed the future?

acid rain: precipitation that has been polluted by acid.

active layer: the layer of permafrost that melts in the summer.

adapt: to make a change in response to new or different conditions.

adaptation: something about a plant or animal that helps it survive in its habitat.

aerate: to create channels that allow air to flow through.

algae: a simple organism found in water that is like a plant but without roots, stems, or leaves.

alpine: high-altitude.

altitude: the height of land above the level of the sea.

amber: hard, fossilized resin. Resin is a sticky substance that oozes from trees.

amplification: magnification.

annual: a plant that flowers and dies in one season. New ones grow the next year from seeds.

aquatic: related to water.

arid: very dry, receiving little rain.

ascend: to climb, move upward.

atmosphere: the blanket of air surrounding the earth.

bacteria: single-celled organisms found in soil, water, plants, and animals, that decay waste. They are often helpful but sometimes harmful.

bedrock: the layer of solid rock under soil.

beneficial: having good or helpful results.

biodegrade: to decay or break down naturally.

biodiversity: the range of living things in an ecosystem.

biological: having to do with something that is or was living.

bioluminescence: a chemical reaction that allows deep-sea creatures to produce their own light.

biome: a large natural area with a distinctive climate, geology, set of water resources, and plants and animals that are adapted for life there.

biosphere: the area of the earth and its atmosphere inhabited by living things.

blubber: an insulating layer of fat underneath an animal's skin that helps keep the animal warm.

boreal forest: another name for the coniferous forest biome.

bountiful: large in quantity.

buoyancy: the ability to float.

burrows: underground holes and tunnels where animals live.

buttresses: thick, aboveground roots that support tall trees.

cache: a collection of things in a place that is hidden or secured.

calcium carbonate: a mineral found in animal bones that forms limestone.

camouflage: the colors or patterns that allow a plant or animal to blend in with its environment.

canopy: an umbrella of trees over the forest.

carnivore: an animal that eats only other animals.

carpet: the mossy forest floor.

carrion: the dead and rotting body of an animal.

centripetal forces: forces that pull a moving object toward a center area.

chlorophyll: a pigment that makes plants green, used in photosynthesis to capture light energy.

circumnavigate: to travel completely around something.

clear-cut logging: a process in which all or almost all the trees in an area are chopped down.

climate: average weather patterns in an area during a period of many years.

climate change: a change in long-term weather patterns, which can happen through natural or man-made processes.

clockwise: the direction that follows the hands of a clock.

closed canopy: when the top branches and leaves of a dense group of trees meet to form a ceiling that light has trouble getting through.

coarse: composed of large particles.

component: a part of something.

compost: decayed food scraps and vegetation that can be put back in the soil.

coniferous: describes cone-bearing shrubs and trees, often with needles for leaves. Coniferous trees do not lose their leaves each year.

conserve: to save or protect something, or to use it carefully so it isn't used up.

consumer: an organism that eats other organisms.

counterclockwise: the direction that goes opposite to the hands of a clock.

cultivation: preparing and using land to grow crops.

current: the steady flow of water or air in one direction.

decay: to break down and rot.

deciduous: plants and trees that shed their leaves each year.

decomposers: bacteria, fungi, and worms that break down wastes and dead plants and animals.

deforestation: the process through which forests are cleared to use land for other purposes.

dense: closely compacted.

desert: the hottest biome, with very little rain, less than 10 inches per year.

desertarium: a small, enclosed desert habitat.

desertification: the transformation of non-desert into desert, usually due to lack of water, deforestation, or overgrazing.

diverse: a large variety.

dominant: stronger or more controlling than another.

dormant: when plants are not actively growing during the winter.

drought: a long period of little or no rain.

dung: solid animal waste.

ecology: the study of the relationship between living things and their environment.

ecoregion: a large area, smaller than a biome, that has its own climate, geology, plants, and animals.

ecosystem: an interdependent community of living and nonliving things and their environment.

ecotone: an area where one biome transitions into another.

element: a basic substance, such as gold or oxygen, made of only one kind of atom.

emergent layer: the top level of trees, which get the most sun, above the canopy.

emission: something sent or given off, such as smoke, gas, heat, or light.

endure: to experience for a long time.

environment: everything in nature, living and nonliving, including plants, animals, soil, rocks, and water.

equator: the imaginary line around the planet halfway between the North and South Poles.

erosion: the gradual wearing away of rock or soil by water and wind.

Eurasia: the land mass of Europe and Asia.

evergreen: a tree that keeps its leaves or needles throughout the year.

extinction: the death of an entire species so that it no longer exists.

fault: a crack in the earth's surface that can cause earthquakes.

fauna: the animal life in an ecosystem.

fertile: rich in nutrients and good for growing plants.

flagging: trees with needles and branches on only one side.

flora: the plant life in an ecosystem.

fluctuation: a change.

food chain: a community of animals and plants where each is eaten by another higher up in the chain.

food web: a network of connected food chains.

foothill: a low hill at the base of a mountain.

fossil: the remains or traces of ancient life, including plants and animals.

fungi: organisms that grow on and feed on rotting things. Plural of fungus.

gaping: an adaptation in which a crocodile opens its mouth to regulate heat.

geological events: earthquakes, volcanic eruptions, and erosion.

geology: the rocks, minerals, and physical structure of an area.

germinate: to begin to grow from a seed.

glacier: an enormous mass of frozen snow and ice that moves across the earth's surface.

global warming: an increase in the average temperature of the earth's atmosphere, enough to cause climate change.

grassland: a large area of land covered with grass.

graze: to eat grass.

greenhouse gas: a gas that traps heat in the earth's atmosphere and contributes to the greenhouse effect and global warming.

habitat: a plant or animal's home, which supplies it with food, water, and shelter.

herbivore: an animal that eats only plants.

herb layer: where berries, herbs, and short bushes grow in the forest.

hibernate: to spend the winter in a deep sleep.

horizon: a layer of soil.

hospitable: welcoming.

humus: decaying organic matter made from dead plant and animal material.

indigenous peoples: people who first inhabited a region.

insulate: to keep the heat in and the cold out.

interdependent: relying on each other.

invasive species: a species that is not native to an ecosystem and rapidly expands to crowd out other species.

invincible: something that cannot be defeated.

krummholz line: the highest altitude where stunted trees grow.

larva: the wormlike stage of an insect's life. The plural is larvae.

latitude: an imaginary line around the earth that runs parallel to the equator. It measures your position on the earth north or south of the equator.

leaf litter: fallen leaves and other dead plant material that is starting to break down.

liana: a woody vine that wraps itself around the trunks and branches of trees in an effort to reach the sunlight.

lichen: a plant-like organism made of algae and fungus that grows on solid surfaces such as rocks or trees.

life zones: ecological communities.

limestone: a kind of rock that forms from the skeletons and shells of sea creatures.

mammal: a type of animal, such as a human, dog, or cat. Mammals are born live, feed milk to their young, and usually have hair or fur covering most of their skin.

marine: found in the ocean or having to do with the ocean.

marsh: an inland area of wet, low land.

midnight zone: the ocean zone where there is no sunlight.

migrate: to move from one environment to another when seasons change.

mineral: a naturally occurring solid found in rocks and in the ground. Rocks are made of minerals. Gold and diamonds are precious minerals.

montane: the mountain zone located below 8,000 feet.

natural resource: a material such as coal, timber, water, or land that is found in nature and is useful to humans.

nectar: a sweet fluid made by flowers that attracts insects.

nocturnal: describes an animal that is active at night instead of during the day.

Northern Hemisphere: the half of the planet north of the equator.

nutrients: substances in food and soil that living things need to live and grow.

omnivore: an animal that eats both plants and animals.

open canopy: when the tops of trees are spaced enough to allow sunlight to filter through.

organic matter: decaying plants and animals.

organism: any living thing, such as a plant or animal.

overgraze: when animals eat plants at a rate faster than the plants can grow back or be replaced by new plants.

overhunting: when an animal is hunted in great numbers, so much that their population falls to low levels. This can cause extinction.

oxymoron: a figure of speech that seems contradictory.

pampas: a term for a temperate grassland in South America, especially Argentina.

parasite: a small insect or other living thing that infects a larger animal and lives off it.

parched: dried out.

pelt: an animal skin.

perennial: a plant that flowers and lives for more than one season.

peril: danger.

permafrost: permanently frozen subsoil and rock just beneath the surface of the ground.

photophores: special organs in the bodies of deep-sea creatures that allow them to produce light.

photosynthesis: the process plants use to turn sunlight, carbon dioxide, and water into food.

pictograph: a picture of a word or idea.

plains: a term for a temperate grassland, primarily used in the United States, but also in Canada.

pleated: folded.

plume: when a material spreads out into a shape that resembles a feather.

poaching: illegal hunting or fishing.

polar: the cold climate zones near the North Pole and South Pole.

pollen: a fine, yellow powder produced by flowering plants. Pollen is spread around by the wind, birds, and insects, and is needed by a flower to make a seed.

pollinate: to transfer pollen from the male parts of the plant to the female parts.

polyps: small creatures that live in colonies and form coral.

porous: full of many little holes so water passes through.

prairie: a term for a temperate grassland, primarily used in Canada, but also in the United States.

precarious: risky or dangerous.

precipitation: the falling to Earth of rain, snow, or any form of water.

predator: an animal or plant that kills and eats another animal.

prehensile: able to grasp things.

prey: an animal that is killed by another for food.

producer: green plants able to make their own food.

prolonged: continuing for longer than usual.

putrid: decaying and smelling bad.

radiate: to spread outward.

radically: drastically; profoundly.

ravenous: starving.

regolith: a layer of loose rock, also called weathered bedrock.

resource: anything people use to take care of themselves, such as water and food.

rotation: turning around a fixed point.

sandstorm: a strong wind carrying clouds of sand with it, especially in a desert.

savanna: a dry, rolling grassland with scattered shrubs and trees.

sheath: a protective cover.

shrub layer: where shrubs and bushes grow in the forest.

silt: particles of fine soil, rich in nutrients.

sorghum: an important cereal crop grown in tropical areas, often used to feed livestock.

species: a group of living things that are closely related and can produce offspring.

starch: a white substance found in plant tissues.

steppe: a term for a temperate grassland in Russia and the Ukraine.

steward: a person who looks after something, such as the environment.

stockpile: to store large amounts of something for later use.

strata: layers of the forest.

subalpine: the mountain zone located at 8,000 to 11,500 feet.

subnivean: the ground area below a layer of snow and above soil.

subsoil: the layer of soil beneath the topsoil.

succulents: plants with thick, fleshy leaves and stems that can store water.

sunlight zone: the ocean zone that sunlight penetrates, where photosynthesis can occur and plants can grow.

supple: flexible and able to bend.

sustain: to provide support.

symbiosis: a relationship between two different species of organisms in which each benefits from the other.

taiga: another name for the coniferous forest biome.

taproot: a root that grows down vertically to make contact with water deep underground.

tectonic plates: large sections of the earth's crust that move on top of the hot, melted layer below.

temperate: climate or weather that is not extreme.

tendon: tissue that connects muscles to bones.

terrarium: a small enclosed habitat.

terrestrial: related to land.

texture: the feel or consistency of a substance.

timberline: also called the treeline, the altitude or limit beyond which trees do not grow in mountains or northern latitudes.

topsoil: the top layer of soil.

torrential: a sudden, violent outpouring.

toxin: a poisonous or harmful substance.

trait: a specific characteristic of an organism.

transformation: a dramatic or extreme change.

transformer: trees that change in winter.

transpiration: the evaporation of water from plants, usually through tiny pores in their leaves called stomata.

tropical rainforest: a biome where it is warm all the time.

Tropic of Cancer: a line of latitude north of the equator, marking the northernmost point at which the sun can appear directly overhead at noon.

Tropic of Capricorn: a line of latitude south of the equator, marking the southernmost point at which the sun can appear directly overhead at noon.

tundra: a treeless Arctic region that is permanently frozen below the top layer of soil.

turf: the grass and the layer of earth held by the grass roots. Can also mean the place someone resides and feels ownership of.

twilight zone: the ocean zone reached by some sunlight, but not enough to allow photosynthesis to occur.

understory: the second layer of the forest, made up of saplings.

ungulate: a mammal with hooves.

valve: a structure that controls the passage of fluid through a tube.

veldt: a term for a temperate grassland in South Africa.

vortex: a rapidly whirling spiral of air or water.

vulnerable: susceptible to emotional or physical harm.

wary: feeling or showing caution about possible dangers.

zone: an area of the ocean based on depth.

Metric Conversions

Use this chart to find the metric equivalents to the English measurements in this book. If you need to know a half measurement, divide by two. If you need to know twice the measurement, multiply by two. How do you find a quarter measurement? How do you find three times the measurement?

English	Metric
1 inch	2.5 centimeters
1 foot	30.5 centimeters
1 yard	0.9 meter
1 mile	1.6 kilometers
1 pound	0.5 kilogram
1 teaspoon	5 milliliters
1 tablespoon	15 milliliters
1 cup	237 milliliters

Resources

MUSEUMS AND NATIONAL PARKS

The Smithsonian Institution
si.edu/explore/science

Yellowstone National Park
nps.gov/yell/learn/photosmultimedia/virtualtours.htm

Virtual Tour of Hawaii Volcanoes National Park
nationalparkstraveler.org/2013/06/
take-virtual-tour-hawaii-volcanoes-national-park-video23427

VIDEOS

Take a virtual fieldtrip to the Amazon rainforest: *youtube.com/watch?v=JEsV5rqbVNQ*

Visit Antarctica with the Adventure Learning Expedition:
youtube.com/watch?v=JEsV5rqbVNQ

Xiuhtezcatl Martinez is a 14-year-old eco-hip-hop artist/climate change warrior:
video.nationalgeographic.com/video/
short-film-showcase/0000014d-e82d-d444-a35f-e92df8780000

Discover more about the unpredictable monster storms:
video.nationalgeographic.com/video/101-videos/
00000165-c429-de15-afef-c73da3c90000

**Find out how NASA's scientists use satellite images and honey bees
to monitor changes in springtime greening rates:**
climate.nasa.gov/climate_resources/41/video-sting-of-climate-change

ARTICLES AND WEBSITES

Meet the top 25 strangest animals in the world. In which biomes do they live?
worldsmostawesome.com/lists/top-25-strangest-animals-in-the-world

Where are the 10 most deadly plants in the world found?
themysteriousworld.com/most-deadliest-plants-in-the-world

QR CODE GLOSSARY

page 6: *youtube.com/watch?v=hIy0ZlyPPDg*

page 11: *census.gov/popclock*

page 23: *study.com/academy/lesson/temperate-deciduous-forests-climate-examples-quiz.html*

page 35: *allaboutbirds.org/mesmerizing-migration-watch-118-bird-
species-migrate-across-a-map-of-the-western-hemisphere*

page 44: *nature.org/greenliving/carboncalculator/index.htm*

page 45: *youtube.com/watch?v=hllU9NEcJyg*

page 62: *animalcognition.org/2015/03/11/the-linguistic-genius-of-prairie-dogs*

page 72: *youtu.be/V8vejjVgIHg*

Resources

QR CODE GLOSSARY (Continued)

page 79: *video.nationalgeographic.com/video/arctic_northpole*

page 87: *blogs.discovermagazine.com/notrocketscience/2012/02/20/flowers-regenerated-from-30000-year-old-frozen-fruits-buried-by-ancient-squirrels/#.W8i5gS-ZPFw*

page 92: *youtu.be/wnPQ2XT8Qvw*

page 99: *water.usgs.gov/edu/earthhowmuch.html*

page 100: *video.nationalgeographic.com/video/oceans-narrated-by-sylvia-earle/oceans-barrier-reef*

page 104: *ecowatch.com/plastic-bali-manta-point-diver-2543541335.html*

page 113: *fws.gov/endangered/?ref=topbar*

page 113: *epa.gov/sites/production/files/2016-08/documents/print_wildfires-2016.pdf*

page 113: *earthobservatory.nasa.gov/images/91556*

page 113: *news.nationalgeographic.com/2018/02/cape-town-running-out-of-water-drought-taps-shutoff-other-cities*

page 113: *realclimate.org/index.php/archives/2018/05/does-global-warming-make-tropical-cyclones-stronger*

page 113: *pbs.org/newshour/science/antarctica-is-losing-ice-twice-as-fast-as-anyone-thought*

ESSENTIAL QUESTIONS

Introduction: What type of biome do you live in?

Chapter 1: How does Earth sustain life?

Chapter 2: How are food chains essential to life on Earth?

Chapter 3: How are living things adapted for life in the coniferous forest?

Chapter 4: Why are tropical rainforests called "the lungs of the planet?"

Chapter 5: What changes will occur if the desert continues to be Earth's fastest growing biome?

Chapter 6: How are grasses and hooved animals adapted to thrive in wide-open spaces?

Chapter 7: What happens when ecosystems change?

Chapter 8: In the interconnected web of life, how do warming temperatures in the Arctic impact the planet?

Chapter 9: What makes mountains different from other biomes?

Chapter 10: How does ocean depth impact biodiversity?

Chapter 11: What have you discovered about Earth's vast interconnections?